The Speeches of
Bishop Henry McNeal Turner

The Speeches *of* Bishop Henry McNeal Turner

The Press, the Platform, and the Pulpit

Edited by
Andre E. Johnson

University Press of Mississippi / Jackson

Margaret Walker Alexander Series in African American Studies

The University Press of Mississippi is the scholarly publishing agency of
the Mississippi Institutions of Higher Learning: Alcorn State University,
Delta State University, Jackson State University, Mississippi State University,
Mississippi University for Women, Mississippi Valley State University,
University of Mississippi, and University of Southern Mississippi.
www.upress.state.ms.us

The University Press of Mississippi is a member
of the Association of University Presses.

First printing 2023
∞

Library of Congress Cataloging-in-Publication Data

Names: Johnson, Andre E., editor.
Title: The speeches of Bishop Henry McNeal Turner : the press, the
platform, and the pulpit / edited by Andre E. Johnson.
Other titles: Margaret Walker Alexander series in African American studies.
Description: Jackson : University Press of Mississippi, [2023] | Series:
Margaret Walker Alexander series in African American studies | Includes
bibliographical references and index.
Identifiers: LCCN 2022056876 (print) | LCCN 2022056877 (ebook) | ISBN
9781496843852 (hardback) | ISBN 9781496843869 (trade paperback) | ISBN
9781496843876 (epub) | ISBN 9781496843883 (epub) | ISBN 9781496843890
(pdf) | ISBN 9781496843906 (pdf)
Subjects: LCSH: Turner, Henry McNeal, 1834–1915—Oratory. | Turner, Henry
McNeal, 1834–1915—Sermons. | African Methodist Episcopal
Church—Bishops. | Speeches, addresses, etc., American—African American
authors—History and criticism. | African American orators. | BISAC:
HISTORY / African American & Black | HISTORY / United States / 20th
Century
Classification: LCC E185.97.T94 A5 2023 (print) | LCC E185.97.T94 (ebook)
| DDC 287/.8092—dc23/eng/20221214
LC record available at https://lccn.loc.gov/2022056876
LC ebook record available at https://lccn.loc.gov/2022056877

British Library Cataloging-in-Publication Data available

Contents

Part Two: 1880–1913

Acknowledgments

Though my name is on the cover of this book, many others helped to make this book a reality. My first shout-out is to my graduate assistant, Kimberley Travers, who has been with the Henry McNeal Turner project from the beginning. Even after finishing her studies at Memphis Theological Seminary and the University of Memphis, she continued to serve as a transcriber, researcher, and editor for this project. I am eternally grateful for her work and commitment to seeing this through.

Second, I need to recognize other graduate assistants and students who worked on this project as transcribers. From the University of Memphis, shout-outs go to Solomon Cochren, StaLynn Davis, Dianna Watkins Dickerson, Bradley Mason, Ayo Morton, and Damariye Smith. From Memphis Theological Seminary, I thank Steven Bell, Darron Fouse, Delicia Henderson, Bruce Holder, Byron Houston, and Paul Watson. In addition, all the Memphis Theological Seminary students who enrolled in the Henry McNeal Turner classes made the classes much better and richer with their presence.

Third, Amanda Nell Edgar, Christi Moss, Craig Stewart, and members of the #WriteOn writing group provided support, feedback, and encouragement. While COVID meant that we could not meet in our normal spot (RP Tracks), we still gathered via Zoom, and their backing was much needed, especially on the days when I did not feel like writing or researching. They held me accountable and encouraged me to #WriteOn!

Fourth, I am appreciative of the institutional support I have received. I thank the faculty, staff, and students in the Department of Communication and Film at the University of Memphis and those at Memphis Theological Seminary. In addition, the College of Communication and Fine Arts at the University of Memphis and the American Academy of Religion provided grant funding for this project.

Fifth, I am grateful to the organizers and reviewers for the National Communication Association, the National Council of Black Studies, the Association for the Study of African American Life and History, the Rhetoric Society of America, the Southern States Communication Association, the African American Intellectual History Society, the Transatlantic Roundtable of Religion and Race, and the Tennessee Communication Association. They allowed me space to present work on Turner and to engage in conversations with others who contributed their thoughts and ideas to my research.

Sixth, a shout-out to the wonderful people at the University Press of Mississippi for believing in this project. I especially appreciate Emily Bandy, who served as my editor on this project, and Ellen Goldlust, who served as my copyeditor.

Last but certainly not least, my Gifts of Life Ministries family allowed me time to travel, write, and research while still serving as their pastor. I am truly a blessed man of God to serve at G'Life. And I thank my wife and partner, Lisa, for her support and for being in my life. Thank you for hanging out with me and Bishop Turner for all these years.

The Speeches of
Bishop Henry McNeal Turner

Introduction: The Oratory of Bishop Henry McNeal Turner

In their critical anthology of African American speeches *Lift Every Voice: African American Oratory, 1787–1900*, Philip S. Foner and Robert James Branham write that oratory "remains a pervasive and important practice in American political and social life." They argue that "oratory is still the basic tool of organizing, the crown of ceremonial observance, the currency of advocacy and deliberation." For them, oratory helps to identify "group interests" and enables those groups to "mobilize for action." Through oratory, they contend, "profound differences may be understood" and "grievances and dissent may be brought face-to-face with audiences responsible for injustice."[1] In their review of African American oratory, Richard W. Leeman and Bernard K. Duffy maintain that "African American orators have been prodigiously eloquent" and that "oratory was an important—perhaps the singularly most important—agency by which African Americans could produce social and political change."[2]

Since before the founding of this country, African Americans' use of oratory and public addresses has been paramount to their survival in a society that has consistently deemed them second-class citizens. Through powerful sermons, speeches, and other spoken-word performances, African Americans have not only comforted and encouraged their own communities but also cast a vision of what America could become. Bishop Henry McNeal Turner (1834–1915) exemplified this tradition and excelled in it.

One contemporary said that "as an orator," Turner "is one of the most forcible and eloquent in the United States. His sentences weigh more than the ordinary language of most men. When speaking, he is very impressive, and carries an audience with him as easily as the wind sweeps the chaff before it. He has the power of taking hold of his audience and chaining their attention to the subject under consideration. He has been considered by many, one of the best if not the best orator of his class in the United States."[3]

Early biographer and friend Mungo M. Ponton noted that no one "spoke more eloquently, more learnedly, more effectively, and enunciated more profoundly the eternal principles of human rights than did Henry McNeal Turner."[4] He was so known for his oratorical prowess that some would change their plans when they discovered that he was coming to town to speak. When the *Christian Recorder*'s C. Conover learned that Turner was coming to preach, Conover put on his Sabbath "fixens" and "wended my way thither to hear and be benefited by the solid and unadulterated word expounded by this eminent divine"[5] After hearing Turner speak at the Emancipation Day Celebration in Augusta, Georgia, in 1866, Robert Kent wrote that the audience "had not expected to hear" "such lofty, eloquent language from a colored man. . . . Even the whites could not conceal their admiration nor restrain the applause due to him, as the best orator of the day."[6]

Those who heard Turner also admired his ability to speak thoroughly on many different subjects even within a single speech. At a Fourth of July celebration, Turner "delivered an able oration, in which he reviewed the History of America from its discovery by Columbus to the present day and was pronounced by white and colored to be the most masterly oration they ever heard."[7] Evelina A. Johnson noted that Turner could "fill and pack any church or hall in [Georgia] with either white or colored," and although her church could "seat two thousand," it too was "too small to handle" all who came to hear Turner speak.[8]

Turner excelled in pulpit oratory. One contemporary called him a "Black Moses."[9] *Harper's Weekly* compared him to famed English evangelist Charles Spurgeon.[10] And the *Phrenological Journal* equated him with noted Congregationalist preacher Henry Ward Beecher, hailing him as the "Beecher of the South."[11] His peers regarded him as a "champion of the pulpit," with congregants "falling around the altar like dead men and women."[12] Many maintained that while in Washington, DC, Turner was the most influential African American.[13] Even when Turner was recovering from smallpox and was not at his best, he preached a eulogy for his friend William Tunion that prompted one listener to write that he had never heard Turner's "reverence more earnest and eloquent and conclusive in discourse." Though this observer believed he lacked the "mind or skill to depict the strain and reasoning" of the sermon, he declared that Turner's sermon would be "remembered by all who heard it."[14]

Turner was also known as a great debater. One of his many accomplishments was the founding of the lyceum at the Israel African Methodist Episcopal (AME) Church in Washington, DC. In keeping with his progressive thinking regarding gender, Turner argued the affirmative position on the question, "Has not a lady equally a right to court a gentleman, as a gentleman has to court a lady?" After more than three hours of arguments and counterarguments, the judges declared Turner the winner.[15]

Turner's powerful oratory led him to preach before integrated revivals and command audiences with senators, congressional leaders, and presidents. His eloquence helped him become the first African American chaplain in the armed forces, a delegate to the Georgia Constitutional Convention, and one of the first Black members of the state legislature. His oratorical powers helped him become his church's presiding elder for Georgia and eventually bishop.

Turner's public career lasted more than sixty years. Many of the documents he produced still survive, but until recently, history has not been kind to Turner.[16] Turner has been the subject of a full-length biography, a full-length treatment analyzing his rhetoric from 1866 to 1895, and a rhetorical history that focuses on his career from 1896 to 1915.[17] But since Turner was one of the premier orators of his generation and a progenitor of what we now understand as the African American oratory tradition, a collection of his speeches is long overdue. Outside of Edwin Redkey's *Respect Black: The Writing and Speeches of Henry McNeal Turner* (which is now out of print), Turner's speeches have not been published.[18] Jean Lee Cole's *Freedom's Witness: The Civil War Correspondence of Henry McNeal Turner* focuses only on the letters Turner wrote while serving as a chaplain in the Civil War.[19] My collection of Turner's writings concentrates exclusively on the letters and essays he published in newspapers and journals.[20]

DISCOVERING VOICE: THE ORATORICAL EDUCATION
OF BISHOP HENRY MCNEAL TURNER

Henry McNeal Turner was born free in Newberry Court House, South Carolina, to Hardy Turner and Sarah Greer Turner on February 1, 1834. After his father's death when Henry was young, his mother and grandmother, Hannah Greer, raised him. Stories shared by Greer proved invaluable to the boy and left an indelible mark on his life, showing him the value and power of storytelling.

Ponton's biography of Turner describes him as a "splendid story teller" who could "call up" stories to suit particular occasions.

> This power . . . made him an interesting talker and also enabled him . . . to rehearse many of those old fireside tales with a weirdness, almost akin to reality. He told these stories as they were told by his suffering people, under the dim glare of a flickering light, when he was a lad: and it was these stories and tales of suffering, or torture and hardships that helped to make him the great champion for human rights he became in after-years—for they fired his heart and stirred his soul.[21]

In calling Turner's ability to tell stories a "power," Ponton points to the African oral tradition's deep well. Many African storytellers use this power, which scholars of the African American rhetorical tradition call Nommo— (the "creative power of the spoken word") to shape and cultivate their stories and presentations.[22] According to rhetorical historian George Lampe, African storytellers

> considered sound to be of importance and they produced an oral tradition aimed at keeping the ears rather than the eyes sharpened. . . . Storytellers artfully combined narratives with song, striking imagery and metaphors, and an exhilarating oral style to bring a folk tale to light. While telling a tale, the storyteller produced sounds and noises to enhance the story. He chanted, mimicked, rhymed, and used his body to create sound and to suggest different characters.[23]

One of the stories that Turner shared throughout his life was about a dream he had when he was "eight or nine years old."[24] In the dream, Turner found himself in front of a large crowd of both Blacks and whites who looked to him for instruction. Turner interpreted the dream as God "marking him" for great things, and he drew on this story for inspiration, especially during difficult times.[25]

Although South Carolina law barred African Americans from attending school or becoming literate, Turner obtained a spelling book and attempted to learn how to read and write with help from sympathetic white community members. However, when other white people discovered these efforts, the lessons immediately stopped. Turner then taught himself with the assistance of a "dream angel":

> I would study with all the intensity of my soul until overcome by sleep at night; then I would kneel down and pray, and ask the Lord to teach me what I was not able to understand myself, and as soon as I would fall asleep an angelic personage would appear with open book in hand and teach me how to pronounce every word that I failed in pronouncing while awake, and on each subsequent day the lessons given me in my dreams would be better understood than any other portions of the lessons. This angelic teacher, or dream teacher, at all events, carried me through the old Webster's spelling book and thus enabled me to read the Bible and hymnbook.[26]

By the time Sarah Turner married Jabez Story and the family moved to Abbeville, South Carolina, Turner had taught himself how to read and write; by the time he was fifteen, he had read the entire Bible five times and had memorized lengthy passages of Scripture. Turner later found employment at a law office, where the attorneys took notice of Turner's "quick mind" and "eagerness to learn." They decided to teach him "arithmetic, astronomy, geography, history, law, and even theology," which he much appreciated. Turner concluded that the lawyers answered his prayers in fulfilling his educational aspirations.[27]

Turner also benefited greatly from the spirituals he heard from the enslaved. Before working at the law office, Turner earned a meager income by working alongside enslaved Africans in South Carolina cotton fields watched over by "harsh overseers." He also worked for Nick Smith, a blacksmith, and Thomas Jackson, a carriage maker. The work songs sung by Turner's fellow laborers came to feed his soul.[28]

These spirituals frequently featured "metaphor, innuendo, and indirection," which Lampe notes enabled enslaved people to "express themselves to one another in the presence of whites." Whereas "the slaveholder may have heard in the songs unmeaning jargon, . . . for slaves, the songs were full of meaning."[29] According to Kerran L. Sanger,

> Slaves used the spirituals to reveal themselves to each other, and to provide an alternative definition of self that challenged white claims. The spirituals, both in the act of singing and in the words of the songs, became a critical

part of countermanding the master's ideology about slaves. This was a form of rhetorical resistance that both limited the slaves' worth to their masters and, more importantly, enabled slaves to refute the very definitions and assumptions on which this psychological oppression was based. As they refuted those definitions, they replaced them with ones of their own making.[30]

While both storytelling and singing shaped Turner's oratory, his rhetoric derived its power primarily from the oratorical style of Black preaching. Stephen Ward Angell notes that Turner and his childhood friends loved "imitating preachers" and "baptizing" each other. Some of Turner's "earliest sermons were addressed to the family cow in the pasture."[31] Turner's preaching style probably drew from the example of a preacher he undoubtedly heard many times, Isaac Cook, who also lived in Newberry Court House and who was described as a very "eloquent and persuasive speaker, . . . looked upon . . . as a great man."[32]

According to one white man who had many years earlier heard Cook preach from Jonah 1:6, "What meanest thou O sleeper, arise and call upon thy God,"

> his description of a sinner in the ark of carnal security, afloat on the storm tossed ocean of life, in danger of going to the bottom, and yet asleep and unconscious of peril, was to my boyish mind indescribably awful. I left the place where the sermon was preached under an irresistible conviction that I had listened to a man of God, and the best thing I could do for myself was to take warning and seek for refuge in Christ as I had been so faithfully exhorted to do.[33]

This experiential rhetorical style fascinated the young Turner. Rather than relying on a literal interpretation of the text, Cook went "beneath the text and extrapolated a spiritual meaning for his audience. He symbolically labeled the audience as Jonah; the boat symbolized the false security that carnal desires provide, the storm became the trials we face in life, and Jonah symbolically represents sinners who need saving."[34]

In 1848, Turner joined the Methodist Episcopal Church, South. His conversion came three years later under the preaching of Methodist missionary Samuel Leard, to whom he subsequently wrote about the experience:

Language is inadequate to express my pleasure at a reception of the letter from one to whom I owe so much, who when I was a wild, reckless boy, in 1851, at the camp meeting just beyond Abbeville Court House S. C., opened to me my sad condition, in one of your masterly sermons, and as a mighty instrument in God's hands led me to the feet of a pardoning Jesus. From 1851 up to this moment I have carried in my breast a grateful heart that God ever gave you to the ministry. I love you while living, will love you when dead, and will love you in heaven.[35]

Turner had previously "cursed" and "got drunk" whenever he could "get whisky," describing himself as "the worse boy at Abbeville Court House." But hearing Leard's "powerful preaching" had "stunned" Turner, and he "fell upon the ground, rolled in the dirt, foamed at the mouth, and agonized under conviction till Christ relieved me by his atoning blood." Two years later, the church licensed the nineteen-year-old Turner to preach. He closed his letter to Leard by writing, "I have preached and worked for God in every position held, from the day I gave you my hand up to the present. I am a poor sinner living upon the mercies of God and would be thankful to be remembered by you at a throne of grace. God, however, has honored me far beyond my merits. God bless you, and may your earthly career terminate amid blessings innumerable!"[36]

In 1856, Turner married Eliza Ann Peacher of Columbia, South Carolina. Her father, a carpenter, was believed to be the "wealthiest colored man in Columbia" at their marriage. Only two of Henry and Eliza's children, John and David, reached adulthood.[37]

By all accounts, Turner was successful in his preaching. When an audience in Macon, Georgia, "heard him quote history, ecclesiastical and profane, some of the white people declared him to be a white man galvanized." Challenged by a man to "expound on the text" of the man's choosing, Turner delivered an impromptu sermon that left the "white citizens well pleased": "an offering was called for and $810 was raised a small fortune in that day."[38]

But because church leaders' belief in Black inferiority meant that the Methodist Episcopal Church, South, would never ordain him as a full member of the clergy, Turner later joined the AME Church, and after a brief stint in Baltimore, he moved with his family to Washington, DC, and became pastor of the Israel AME Church, located within walking distance of the US

Capitol. Turner spent hours there, listening to debates and arguments in the House of Representatives and the Senate and learning the art of delibera-tive oratory. Turner started a lyceum at the Israel Church and served as its president, participating in debates about many issues of the day.[39]

While at the Israel AME Church, Turner began to understand the "differ-ence between a speech and an oration."[40] In the words of Kenneth Greenberg,

> Speeches can have many different forms and purposes. They can be used to inform an audience or to arouse it to action. They can be used to sub-tly persuade or viciously to malign. Orations, in terms of their content, can also be used for these purposes, often making them hard to distinguish from speeches. What is different about an oration was that one of its primary func-tions was to inspire respect, even awe for the speaker in the minds of the lis-teners. An oration, in contrast to a speech, was the public display of a superior personality. Orations allowed statesmen to display their independence, as well as their superior intelligence and virtue.[41]

In short, orations typically "create an air of credibility and respect for the speaker," using performance to create a persona with a "superior personal-ity."[42] According to Ponton, Turner "used a great many gestures" and "had the magnetism of the orator. He could entertain his audience for hours at the time. He was persuasive and eloquent" and "was never without an engage-ment to perform some useful service, not only to his own Church but to all Churches and his race in general."[43] Turner's oratorical persona established him as a rhetorical leader not only within the AME Church but outside of it as well.

As with any anthology of speeches, the compilation of *The Speeches of Bishop Henry McNeal Turner: The Press, the Platform, and the Pulpit*, involved answering several questions: How am I going to present this material? Should I present all of the speeches in their entirety, or should I edit them? How much annotation should I include? I would have liked to offer these speeches in their extant form, without any omissions, but the lengthy nature of many of the speeches made doing so impractical. Space considerations also dictated that some speeches could not be included at all. Thus, this volume is a selected and edited collection of Turner's addresses.

I obtained the texts included in this volume from many different sources—among them newspapers, books, and pamphlets—and there is no way to confirm their accuracy. The speeches, of course, were not recorded, and no stenographer provided a word-for-word transcription of what Turner said. But these accounts of his words are the rhetorical artifacts that people read, and they consequently operated as representations of Turner's oratory. They are thus worthy of study.

I have retained the original spelling, grammar, punctuation, capitalization, and paragraph indentation. Parenthetical remarks regarding the audience's response to Turner's words have been silently omitted; all other omissions are indicated by ellipses. Other editorial interventions are enclosed in square brackets. Also, for texts originally published in newspapers, I have used the titles given at that time. In other cases, I have added titles.

Part 1 of the volume consists of Turner's speeches from 1862 to 1879, and Part 2 features Turner's speeches from 1880 to 1913. I present the writings in chronological order within each section, with the title, date delivered, and publication date.

Notes

1. Philip S. Foner and Robert James Branham, eds., *Lift Every Voice: African American Oratory, 1787–1900* (Tuscaloosa: University of Alabama Press, 1998), 1.

2. Richard W. Leeman and Bernard K. Duffy, *The Will of a People: A Critical Anthology of Great African American Speeches* (Carbondale: Southern Illinois University Press, 2012), 5–6.

3. William J. Simmons, *Men of Mark: Eminent, Progressive, and Rising* (Cleveland: Rewell, 1887), 818.

4. Mungo M. Ponton, *Life and Times of Henry M. Turner* (Atlanta: Caldwell, 1917), 24.

5. C. Conover, "Washington Correspondence," *Christian Recorder*, April 4, 1863.

6. Robert F. Kent, "Letter from Augusta," *Christian Recorder*, January 27, 1866.

7. M. G. Saunders, "Highly Interesting from Georgia," *Christian Recorder*, July 21, 1866.

8. Evelina A. Johnson, "H. M. Turner and His Bulletin," *Christian Recorder*, November 2, 1872.

9. Thadeus Edgar Horton, "A Black Moses," in *Afro-American Encyclopedia*, ed. James T. Haley (Nashville, TN: Haley and Florida, 1895), 35–38.

10. "Rev. H. M. Turner," *Harper's Weekly*, December 13, 1863.

11. "Henry M. Turner, D.D., The Eminent Colored Preacher of the South," *Phrenological Journal and Life Illustrated* 61, no. 2 (August 1875): 84.

12. Thomas C. Hinton, "From Washington," *Christian Recorder*, July 4. 1863; Thomas C. Hinton, "Washington Correspondence," *Christian Recorder*, October 3, 1863.

13. Thomas C. Hinton. "From Washington," *Christian Recorder*, July 4, 1863.

14. Thomas C. Hinton. "Washington Correspondence," *Christian Recorder*, May 14, 1864.

15. Thomas C. Hinton. "Washington Correspondence," *Christian Recorder*, August 8, 1863.

16. Andre E. Johnson, *The Forgotten Prophet: Bishop Henry McNeal Turner and the African American Prophetic Tradition* (Lanham, MD: Lexington Books, 2012), 3.

17. Stephen Ward Angell, *Bishop Henry McNeal Turner and African American Religion in the South* (Knoxville: University of Tennessee Press, 1992); Andre E. Johnson, *Forgotten Prophet*; Andre E. Johnson, *No Future in This Country: The Prophetic Pessimism of Bishop Henry McNeal Turner* (Jackson: University Press of Mississippi, 2020).

18. Henry McNeal Turner, *Respect Black: The Writing and Speeches of Henry McNeal Turner*, comp. and ed. Edwin Redkey (New York: Arno, 1971).

19. Henry McNeal Turner, *Freedom's Witness: The Civil War Correspondence of Henry McNeal Turner*, ed. Jean Lee Cole (Morgantown: West Virginia University Press, 2013).

20. Andre E. Johnson, ed., *An African American Pastor before and during the American Civil War*, 6 vols. (New York: Mellen, 2010–18).

21. Ponton, *Life and Times*, 86; Andre E. Johnson, *Forgotten Prophet*, 21.

22. For the study of Nommo, see Arthur L. Smith (Molefi Asante), "Markings of an African Concept," *Today's Speech* 19, no. 2 (spring 1971): 13–18; Adetokunbo F. Knowles-Borishade, "Paradigm for Classical African Orature," *Journal of Black Studies* 21, no. 4 (1991): 488–501; Maulana Karenga, "Nommo, Kawaida, and Communicative Practice: Bringing Good into the World," in *Understanding African American Rhetoric*, ed. Ronald L. Jackson and Elaine B. Richardson (New York: Routledge, 2003), 3–22; Lynn Clark, "Talk about Talk," *Journal of Speculative Philosophy* 18, no. 4 (2004): 317–25; Sheena C. Howard. "Manifestations of Nommo: Afrocentric Analysis of President Barack Obama," *Journal of Black Studies* 42, no. 5 (2011): 737–50; Vorris Nunley, *Keepin' It Hushed: The Barbershop and African American Hush Harbor Rhetoric* (Detroit: Wayne State University Press, 2011); Damariye L. Smith, "Kemetic Principles in African American Public Address: An Interrogation of the Rhetoric of Joseph C. Price and the Kemetic Tradition," *Journal of Black Studies* 51, no. 5 (2020): 458–80.

23. George Lampe, *Frederick Douglass: Freedom's Voice, 1818–1845* (East Lansing: Michigan State University Press, 1998), 3–4.

24. D. W. Culp, *Twentieth Century Negro Literature* (Naperville, IL: Nichols, 1902), 42.

25. Angell, *Bishop Henry McNeal Turner*, 9.

26. Simmons, *Men of Mark*, 807.

27. Simmons, *Men of Mark*, 807; Minton J. Batton, "Henry McNeal Turner, Negro Bishop Extraordinary," *Church History* 8 (1938): 232; Andre E. Johnson, *Forgotten Prophet*, 17–18; Angell, *Bishop Henry McNeal Turner*, 10.

28. Andre E. Johnson, *Forgotten Prophet*, 17; Angell, *Bishop Henry McNeal Turner*, 8.

29. Lampe, *Frederick Douglass*, 5.

30. Kerran L. Sanger, "Slave Resistance and Rhetorical Self-Definition: Spiritual as a Strategy," *Western Journal of Communication* 59, no. 3 (1995): 179.

31. Angell, *Bishop Henry McNeal Turner*, 9.

32. Andre E. Johnson, *Forgotten Prophet*, 22–23.

33. Stephen W. Angell, "Black Methodist Preachers in the South Carolina Upcountry, 1840–1866: Isaac (Counts) Cook, James Porter, and Henry McNeal Turner," in *Ain't Gonna*

Lay My 'Ligion Down: African American Religion in the South, ed. Alonzo Johnson and Paul Jersild (Columbia: University of South Carolina Press, 1996), 94.

34. Andre E. Johnson, *Forgotten Prophet*, 23.

35. W. P. Harrison, *The Gospel among the Slaves: A Short Account of Missionary Operations among the African Slaves of the Southern States* (Nashville, TN: Publishing House of the M.E. Church, South, 1893), 379.

36. Harrison, *Gospel among the Slaves*, 380.

37. Andre E. Johnson, *Forgotten Prophet*, 18.

38. Andre E. Johnson, *Forgotten Prophet*, 19.

39. Andre E. Johnson, *Forgotten Prophet*, 19–20.

40. Andre E. Johnson, *Forgotten Prophet*, 23.

41. Kenneth Greenberg, *Masters and Statesmen: The Political Culture of American Slavery* (Baltimore: Johns Hopkins University Press, 1985), 12.

42. Andre E. Johnson, *Forgotten Prophet*, 24.

43. Ponton, *Life and Times*, 128.

Part One

—•—

1862–1879

Introduction

Henry McNeal Turner initially thought that the idea of civil war was "insane" and "wicked." Writing in his journal on May 13, 1861, he noted his belief that supporters of the war had failed to think about its "cost" and ramifications. He admonished supporters to remember that there was a "hell and a God," and he hoped that God would "help the people to think before they are beyond the reach of thought."[1]

However, when he arrived at the Israel African Methodist Episcopal (AME) Church in 1861, his position had changed. Turner ultimately became one of the leading supporters of the war effort and one of the strongest advocates for African American participation. His support and advocacy were evident not only in the press but also from the pulpit. Writing for the *Atlantic* magazine in 1873, Sidney Andrews noted that "preach from what text he would, begin where he might," Turner "seemed to always find the war within the scope of his theme."[2]

While many of Turner's preaching texts have been lost to history, some examples of his preaching ministry remain. Part 1 starts with two sermons—one from 1862 and the other from 1863. I have titled the first one "In the Beginning God Created," and in it Turner spoke of Creation not as a thing of the past but as a current phenomenon. Foreshadowing some of the tenets of process theology, Turner maintained that God's Creation was ongoing. In the second sermon, "The Colored Men and the Draft," Turner blamed the country's turmoil on animosity between white and Black people and challenged his congregation to remove the murder in their hearts and search within to find the will to love their enemies and pray for their persecutors.

When Turner arrived in Augusta, Georgia, in December 1865, organizers of the First Anniversary of Freedom asked him to deliver the January 1, 1866, Emancipation Day Speech, which launched his political career. Turner celebrated the Union victory and argued that both Blacks and whites should let "by-gones be by-gones." Turner optimistically suggested that Blacks and whites could work together in the South and help build a better nation. Through mutual respect, prejudice would "melt away," replaced by unity and brother- and sisterhood.

But such visions came to a crashing halt two years later. In the wake of Turner's efforts to build the Republican Party in Georgia and his service on the state constitutional committee in June 1868, the people of Bibb County elected him to the Georgia House of Representatives. Just two months later, however, conservatives introduced a bill to deny African Americans the right to serve in the legislature because the new state constitution did not explicitly give them the right to hold office.

In response, Turner addressed the body on September 3, delivering what many observers call his finest speech. Commonly called "I Claim the Rights of a Man," Turner's "On the Eligibility of Colored Members to Seats in the Georgia Legislature" is probably one of the finest orations in American history. With his witty sarcasm and bitter invectives, Turner's use of prophetic disputation (offering another speaker's words and then addressing them directly) exposed the hypocrisy and anti-Black thought of the conservatives.[3] Understanding that the result was a foregone conclusion, Turner closed with an ominous warning: "You may expel us, gentlemen, by your votes, today; but, while you do it, remember that there is a just God in heaven, whose All-Seeing Eye beholds alike the acts of the oppressor and the oppressed, and who, despite the machinations of the wicked, never fails to vindicate the cause of Justice, and the sanctity of His own handiwork."

Turner's political career was not limited to electoral politics. Turner was a prime mover in the Colored Conventions movement.[4] Starting in 1830, the Colored Conventions gave African Americans space and place to voice their opinions and concerns about the issues and problems many faced daily. Delegates promoted the ideas of equal treatment under the law, suffrage, temperance, education, and moral reform.

Two weeks after his expulsion from the Georgia House, Turner called for an October 1868 state convention for the "purpose of taking into consideration our condition and determining upon the best course of action." Turner argued that African Americans' "personal liberty [was] in great danger," along with their "civil and political rights," and reasoned that the same "power" that "overrode the constitution in one thing, [would] do it in another."[5]

At the National Colored Convention in Washington, DC, the following year, the convention named Turner its temporary chair. In a brief speech, Turner thanked the attendees and reminded them why they were there. "The cause for which we have met is more than noble," Turner proclaimed, "our object is divine, and God will crown it with success, sooner or later. Manhood rights [are] all we want, South, North, East and West."

The lobbying efforts by Turner and others seemed to pay off. Congress passed the "Georgia Bill," which placed the state under military jurisdiction and required the adoption of the Fifteenth Amendment as a condition for readmission to the Union. When the state ratified the amendment under a bill of reorganization, Turner was pleased. In his "Speech on the Fifteenth Amendment," Turner celebrated the passage in the "high" or "grand style" of nineteenth-century oratory, describing the amendment as "the finish of our national fabric; it is the headstone of the world's asylum; the crowning event of the nineteenth century; the brightest glare of glory that ever hung over land or sea. Hereafter, the oppressed children of all countries can find a temple founded upon gratitude and religious equity, ample enough to accommodate them all." Turner went on to proclaim the amendment an "ensign of our citizenship, the prompter of our patriotism, the bandage that is to blind-fold Justice while his sturdy hands holds the scales and weighs out impartial equity to all, regardless of popular favor or censure. It is the ascending ladder for the obscure and ignoble to rise to glory and renown, the well of living water never to run dry, the glaring pillar of fire in the night of public commotion, and the mantling pillar of cloud by day to repel the scorching rays of wicked prejudice."

Just as the optimism of his 1866 Emancipation Day speech soon was replaced by disappointment, his high hopes for the passage of the Fifteenth Amendment gave way to frustration as southern whites nullified the spirit of the amendment meant to give African American men the right to vote. White conservatives reclaimed control of both houses of the state legislature through voter intimidation tactics and outright vote stealing in the 1870 elections. Two years later, white conservatives won by even larger margins, effectively ending Reconstruction efforts in Georgia.

By then, however, Turner had begun to focus his attention on building the AME Church in Georgia, serving as presiding elder for the state. In a speech that I have titled "Resignation as Presiding Elder," Turner reminded listeners that in a single year, he had "traveled over fifteen thousand miles" within Georgia, "organizing and planting Churches, and superintending the work, together," as well as speaking "over five hundred times." At the same time, he had been organizing the Republican Party and working for its "maintenance and perpetuity as no other man in the State has": he had "put more men in the field, made more speeches, organized more Union Leagues, political associations, clubs and [had] written more campaign documents that received larger circulation than any other man in the State."

After Turner resigned as presiding elder at the beginning of 1872, the AME Church assigned him to pastor Savannah's St. Philip AME Church. Serving as a pastor gave Turner time not only to rest and recuperate from his travels but also to write and give lectures. One of the first was "On the Present Duties and Future Destiny of the Negro Race," delivered on September 2, 1872, at St. Philip in front of the Savannah Lyceum Association. Turner argued that African Americans needed to seek out a liberal education so that they could become writers of history and orators who could provide guidance along the path to a great and glorious African American future.

On April 8, 1873, at Savannah's Second Baptist Church, Turner delivered "The Negro in All Ages." In this speech, Turner engaged in "didactic oratory," designed to "transform its audience by way of teaching" and by "presenting new facts to the audience that would serve as foundations for understanding and learning." Turner navigated the intersections of race and religion, adopting a prophetic persona to refute much of the science of the day that was detrimental to African American identity.[6]

Turner returned to the grand or high style of eloquence in his "Eulogy of Charles Sumner," delivered on March 18, 1874, at St. Philip AME Church. Using rhetorical figures such as amplification, anaphora, and figurative language, Turner evoked emotion by celebrating Massachusetts senator's life and legacy moved the audience to support the civil rights bill that Congress was debating at the time. Turner told the congregation that his good friend Sumner was

[t]oo noble to do wrong, too great to be mean, too wise to make a blunder, too high to countenance a low act, too solid to be a trickster, too pure to be a politician, too just to be partial, too brave to cower before men or devils, too spotless to be slandered in the most calumnious age the world ever witnessed, armed with the helmet of right, and panoplied with a code of principles, as irreversible as the flowing current of the Mississippi river, he stood out as grand and as majestic before the world as thundering Sinai did, when the shuddering hosts of Israel trembled at its base. A vital amazement, an intellectual prodigy, a human creature with superhuman traits, such was Sumner, the man of destiny, molded out of the matrix of heaven by the command of God, to front the reformatory measures born in the middle of the nineteenth century, and well did he do the work assigned. What staggered Hale and disheartened Chase, only fired the soul of the great Sumner.

The following year, Turner joined other African Americans in Augusta at the Georgia Convention of Colored Men, which had been called in response to white violence against the Black community. Prior to the massacre, there had been rumors that African Americans planned an insurrection in central Georgia. In response to the unfounded allegations, white mobs shot, whipped, clubbed, and stabbed Black people. On October 8, 1875, Turner delivered the "Report of the Committee on Resolutions," not only denying the charge but also calling the "malicious rumor" an attempt to enable white people to "expend their diabolical hate in murderous assaults upon the colored race." If nothing was going to be done about this atrocity, they advised Black people to leave their counties and necessary the state.

Six weeks later, on November 28, Turner delivered a sermon at St. James' Tabernacle in Savannah, Georgia that I have titled "Thou God Seest Me." Drawing from the story of Hagar (Genesis 16:13), Turner centers his sermon on the phrase, "God seest me," telling his listeners that that since God saw Hagar in the wilderness, God would see them too.

On January 2, 1876, Turner delivered another sermon, "This Year Thou Shalt Die," at St. James' Tabernacle. Drawing from Jeremiah 28:16, Turner reminded congregants that despite the jubilant feelings and expectations that the new year brings, some of them might not live to see the end of the year. The sermon is a call to recognize that death comes and sometimes comes quickly.

Later in the year, Turner served as a delegate to the 1876 Republican National Convention, hoping to reignite the spirit of the earlier radicalism of the party. Appreciating his work in Georgia, convention planners offered Turner the opportunity to second the presidential nomination of James G. Blaine, a US senator and former House Speaker from Maine. In his "Nomination Speech for James G. Blaine," Turner extolled the candidate's virtues, arguing that Blaine stood as the "champion of Republican principles." Blaine had originated the "spirit of the fourteenth amendment" and had stood by Lincoln during the "great struggle this country was passing through for freedom and justice and equality to all mankind." Turner closed by reminding his audience that after the Democrats had won the previous election, Blaine "shook aloft the banner of the Republican party, united the party, and defied the Democracy of this nation, and breathed again the spirit of activity and hope into this prostrate Republican party."

With the Compromise of 1877 effectively ending Reconstruction, many Black people at the grassroots level began to reconsider the possibility of emigration. In 1878, one company that attempted to address this opportunity, the Liberian Exodus Joint Stock Steamship Company, purchased the *Azor* to take emigrants from Charleston, South Carolina, to Monrovia, Liberia. Turner was among those who welcomed the ship to Charleston, offering blessings and support. In his "Consecration Speech of the *Azor*," Turner argued to rousing applause that the vessel "stands as a monument to the genius, manhood, and love of race of the Negro, and silences his calumniators who said that he could do nothing."

While Turner supported emigration, many members of his church did not. With grassroots support for emigration growing and a desire to refute church leaders' arguments against it, Turner developed his own theory of emigration and prepared to explain it in an address to the 1879 National Conference of Colored Men of the United States, which was held in Nashville, Tennessee. When church duties prevented Turner from attending, he sent three hundred copies of his "Emigration of the Colored People of the United States." Although his words were not included in the convention minutes, I include the speech here because he probably would have been allowed to deliver it had he attended and because it was in high demand: Turner had a pamphlet version printed and sold one thousand copies for ten cents each.

"Emigration of the Colored People of the United States" contains Turner's first full-throated argument for emigration and offers three primary reasons for doing so. First, African Americans should take pride in their homeland.

Second, Africa's land and climate offered some of the best advantages for planting and farming. Finally, Turner predicted that "bad times" were ahead for America—and even worse times for African Americans.

NOTES

1. Andre E. Johnson, *No Future in This Country: The Prophetic Pessimism of Bishop Henry McNeal Turner* (Jackson: University Press of Mississippi, 2020), 68.

2. Sidney Andrews, "Israel Bethel Church," *Atlantic Monthly*, December 1873, 727–37.

3. Andre E. Johnson, *The Forgotten Prophet: Henry McNeal Turner and the African American Prophetic Tradition* (Lanham, MD: Lexington Books, 2012), 12.

4. For more on the Colored Conventions movement, see P. Gabrielle Foreman, Jim Casey, and Sarah Lynn Patterson, eds., *The Colored Conventions Movement: Black Organizing in the Nineteenth Century* (Chapel Hill: University of North Carolina Press, 2021). See also the Colored Conventions website, https://coloredconventions.org/.

5. Andre E. Johnson, "Further Silence upon Our Part Would Be an Outrage: Bishop Henry McNeal Turner and the Colored Conventions Movement," in *Colored Conventions Movement*, ed. Foreman, Casey, and Patterson, 303.

6. Andre E. Johnson, "'Is the Negro Like Other People?': Race, Religion, and the Didactic Oratory of Henry McNeal Turner," in *Converging Identities: Blackness in the Modern African Diaspora*, ed. Julius O. Adekunle and Hettie V. Williams (Durham, NC: Carolina Academic Press, 2013), 212.

In the Beginning God Created

Delivered at the Israel African Methodist Episcopal Church,
Washington, DC, 1862

SOURCE: Sidney Andrews, "Israel Bethel Church," *Atlantic Monthly* 32,
no. 194 (December 1873): 727–37

*In 1873, white journalist Sidney Andrews published this account of his visit to
Israel Bethel Church more than a decade earlier. Drawing from Genesis 1:1, "In
the beginning God created the heaven and the earth," Turner spoke of Creation
as ongoing.*

[Turner] had heard men argue, he said, "that this record of the beginning of
things is not true; that there was more than one source of life on the earth;
that we did not all descend from Adam and the garden of Eden; that no well-
educated person now accepted what was said in the first chapter of the Bible
as an exact statement of fact. All this sort of talk, friends, need not trouble
us. The Bible is true: on that I rest my feet. Whether we always understand
the Bible right, is another thing. We must all study it as faithfully as we can.
The Lord will not hold us responsible for mistakes, if we really do the best
we know how. He is a tender father, we are ignorant children." . . .

"This is what God means,— the wisest, greatest, highest, most majestic,
most loving, most tender. All nations have this something above all other

things. That is God. He created the heavens and the earth and the sea and all that is therein. He is manifested to us in Christ, the Captain of our Salvation." Some one in the rear of the church shouted out, "Thank God for the Captain!" To which the preacher responded, "Yes, thank God for the Captain! God is so high and mighty that we poor creatures would not have dared to call him 'Father,' except for the Captain who redeemed us and will lead us on to glorious victory. The Lord Jesus was in heaven just as God was, but he couldn't bear to have the sons of men so far away, and therefore he came down to earth, took our form, lived our life, and suffered everything to death, that he might know just how to be the Captain of our Salvation. He did not escape anything. He was naked and hungry and thirsty and shut in prison, just as we have been. That was what God created him in the heavens for in the beginning, to know whatever afflicts us, so that he might be our Captain."

"In the beginning God created, the Bible says. God has beginnings every day, and he goes on creating every day. Shall I tell you what? He is making us poor men over every day of all this war time. We weren't worth much two years ago; perhaps we aren't worth a great deal now; but God will make men and women of us before he rests from his work. He is every day creating righteousness of heart among the white people of this land, and when he finishes that creation the chains will fall from our race, and we shall walk free everywhere and know no master but Christ. And he is every day creating friends for us, not only here in Washington, but all over the North. Whoever else goes back on him, we can't do so!"

The Colored Men and the Draft

Delivered at the Israel African Methodist Episcopal Church, Washington, DC, August 16, 1863

SOURCE: *Christian Recorder*, August 29, 1863

The Christian Recorder *reprinted this account of Turner's sermon on Psalm 85:8 ("I will hear what God the Lord will speak; for he will speak peace unto his people, and to his saints; but let them not turn again to folly.") from the* Washington National Republican, *August 18, 1863.*

[Psalm 85 was] written just after the children of Israel were delivered from the seventy years' captivity in Babylon. Having felt the judgments of God, that people were now willing to hear what God would speak to them. They had suffered years of captivity with all its degradation, toil, and wo, and they were thus sufficiently humiliated to become willing to listen to God's voice. In times of trouble we have many advisers. Some will tell you this will relieve you; others, that will relieve you. But no rule of conduct will give such success as God's rules. None will lead in the right way, save the mighty word of God. We are prone to follow our own devices, but this is mixed with corruption, and leads us astray. Prone to wickedness, we love that which is false and wicked. Thus we waste our lives in this world instead of looking to God, and following his advice. Turn to God and hear what he has to say, and perfect peace will come.

God often sends affliction upon us for our good. Our sick beds, the death of our friends, and the affliction of our bodies are all designed to humble our pride and work for our highest good. So with national chastisements. This great and mighty nation has been full of wickedness. We are being punished. Bloodshed and all the horrors and devastations of war are abroad in the land. It is estimated that over 300,000 souls have gone down to dust during this war. Yet we have not reformed. We are not humbled. Our churches, both white and colored, are even more indifferent than ever amid this dire affliction, while thousands are going down to the grave and to eternal death. What is the matter? The voice of God has not been listened to. All our sorrows are the fruits of sin. We must repent. Individuals cannot be saved without repentance. Nations must repent. The high and mighty as well as the poorest must get down in the dust of humility and repentance before God, or they cannot be saved. We are all disposed to find fault with others and blame them for our troubles. We are constantly pulling the mote out of our brother's eye.

We must love our enemies. There is too much hatred in this land, and God will never deliver us while we cherish such hellish feelings. Look at this nation. We are hating each other. The dominant, or white race, are hating us, and abusing us, every opportunity, heaping upon our heads indignities of every kind, and even murdering in cold blood, as they did in New York.[1] And we, in turn, have the same revengeful feeling toward the white race. Think you, my brethren, we can ever obtain the favor of God, with the blessings of peace as a nation, while he witnesses such murder in our hearts, as many of us now cherish? We have got to put away these abominations. It is the cause of our troubles. We have been cherishing the feeling of hatred, until we have gone to butchering each other by the thousands. We must love our enemies and pray for them which despitefully use and persecute us.

But an affliction has come upon us greater than all others. Many of our people are in mourning over the draft. [Turner] felt a wish to comfort them

---

1. Probably a reference to events in New York City on July 13–16, 1863. After Congress passed new laws regarding the Civil War draft, white men took to the streets in a protest that quickly turned into a riot targeting the Black community. Rioters attacked and burned businesses and schools and lynched eleven Black men. See Leslie M. Harris, *In the Shadow of Slavery: African Americans in New York City, 1862–1863* (Chicago: University of Chicago Press, 2003).

in this sorrow. Hearts of mothers, sisters, and friends were bowed in sadness. Has anything served to humble us more than this? We needed this affliction. The war has gone on for nearly three years, and our people have been enjoying it. Many have forgotten the church of God, and gone away to mix in sin, swearing, and breaking God's holy day. . . . We, as colored people, have been praying for the dawn of this very day. We have even been shouting the year of jubilee, when liberty has been proclaimed to the captive. Just as our prayers are being answered, just as victory is dawning, just as God is about to deliver us, we hear the hoarse voice of murmuring and complaint. You are just like the people of Israel, who, though delivered by the wonderful power of God from Egyptian bondage, murmured at God and his servant Moses.

Shall we not take the bitter with the sweet? In all parts of this afflicted country families have been broken—fathers, husbands, and sons have been stricken down, and mourning and desolation have gone into thousands of families. But our race has been free from these afflictions. We have been rejoicing while the whole land has been mourning. Thousands of our people have tasted the precious sweets of freedom. The Colored Churches of this city, in all our meetings, have rung with our hallelujahs and our rejoicings over what God has done for our people. But a short time ago we were full of enthusiasm, and the very arches of heaven rang with our loud hurrahs in our war meetings. Now the scene is changed. Some of our people complain because they are compelled to go and help maintain and preserve our country. Some have even blamed your preacher and others, as the cause of your being drafted.

Am I the President of the United States? Can I go to the War Department and give orders? Or perhaps I went to Congress, and they passed the enrolment act just to please me. I beg of you, my brethren, not to be so foolish. "Let them not turn again to folly." [Turner] had been made sick when he heard his people, some of whom had themselves been made free by it, say they were opposed to the war! Why, Copperhead Seymour[2] could say no more than that! Our people should all be in favor of the war until our race is free, God shall be honored, and the rebellion put down. Don't grumble; if you do, you insult God and put an everlasting stain on your posterity. God will surely speak peace when His work, which this affliction is designed to

2. Horatio Seymour (1810–86) served two terms (1852–54 and 1863–65) as governor of New York and was the 1868 Democratic nominee for president, losing to Ulysses S. Grant.

produce, is accomplished. Then the millennium will dawn. Our race, that has been afflicted and down-trodden, shall then stand still and see the salvation of the Lord. For our little privations now, remember that thousands of our race will be free and enjoy their God-given rights. God is already doing more for us than we deserve. Instead, then, of fault-finding, go to Him with hearts of humility and gratitude. Praise Him for what He has done and give your lives to His service.

Emancipation Day Speech

Delivered at the Springfield Baptist Church, Augusta, Georgia,
January 1, 1866

SOURCE: *Celebration of the First Anniversary of Freedom* (Augusta:
Loyal Georgian, 1866)

*This Emancipation Day Speech, delivered on the "first anniversary of freedom,"
served as Turner's reintroduction to the state of Georgia. In this four-part oration,
Turner addressed a wide range of topics, among them celebration, the American
covenant with God, slavery and black heroism in the Civil War, and the need
for freedom and harmony between African Americans and white Americans.*

Gentlemen and Ladies, or Fellow Citizens, I should have said, we have assembled to-day under circumstances, unlike those of any other day in the history
of our lives. We have met for the purpose of celebrating this, the first day
of the New Year, not because it is the first New Year's Day we ever saw, but
because it is the first one we ever enjoyed. O! how different this day from
similar days of the past. The first day of January hitherto, was one of gloom
and fearful suspense. The foundation of our social comforts hung upon
the scales of apprehension, and fate with its decisions of weal or wo looked
every one of us in the face, and dread forebodings kept in dubious agitation,
every fleeting moment that passed. But to-day we stand upon no such sandy

foundation. Uncertainty is no more the basis of our existence; we have for our fulcrum the eternal principles of right and equity.

Associated with the first day of January are peculiar interests, which in their accommodation to the world of colored men, will hereafter enshrine it in their affections with a deathless sacredness, forever and ever. This day which hitherto separated so many families, and tear-wet so many faces; heaved so many hearts, and filled the air with so many groans and sighs; this of all others the most bitter day of the year to out poor miserable race, shall henceforth and forever be filled with acclamations of the wildest joy, and expressions of ecstasy too numerous for angelic pens to note. Before this day, all other days will dwindle into insignificance with us, and the glory that shall environ it, will, compared with which, make hazy in appearance all other days God's day excepted. It has been the custom of men in all ages to celebrate certain days in commemoration of certain achievements or national transactions. A few out of the many which are observed in some manner, are days which hold universal claim upon the observance of all men, and among them we may mention the Sabbath, and Christmas. True, the observance of those two heaven consecrated days, follow only in the wake of religious civilization, while all nations civilized or pagans, have their regular anniversaries, be the cause of the observance fictitious or real. But reverting to the customs of civilized nations, we will only name a few. The Sabbath day demands our attention first of all, in noticing those reckoned in the sacred catalogue. This day was hallowed and set apart by God himself, to be observed by all the inhabitants of the earth as a day of rest and of gratitude to God for the marvelous act which his Almighty fiat performed, in standing out upon the unfathomable abyss of an eternal nonentity, and decorating the dismal caverns of old chaos with burning solars and rolling worlds. This act of Almighty greatness and wisdom, at first called forth the undying praises of the skies, and God perpetuated its sanctity on earth by hallowing the day of its final completion. That day remained sacred in the hearts of mankind for four thousand years. At the end of which time, God clothed his Son,—the brightest jewel that glittered in the courts of Heaven—in the garb of humanity, and He left that throne for a while, which had not been vacated since the morn of eternity, and came to earth with his eternal attributes circumbounded by flesh and blood, endured a miserable life; died an ignominious death; robed death, hell, and the grave of their visionary trophies; and on the first day of the week rose from the dead to the joy of earth and ecstacy of Heaven, and changed the sanctity of the day, by virtue of the greater feat performed, from the seventh to the first day of the week, and for over eighteen hundred years, Christians of every tongue and every clime have kept it as a day of gratitude to Heaven for the triumphs of Emmanuel. This day above all others, holds the first claim upon all men irrespective of class or condition, a day upon which is stamped fadeless perpetuity.

2d. The next day which was important in the history of the civilized world was the first day of the year of Jubilee. Theologians have differed it is true, as to whether the claims of the jubilee were national or universal, whether its special bearings contemplated only the house of Israel, or religious humanity at large. However, on the day of its arrival, the blast of the trumpet and the blow of the rams horn, sent a thrill of universal joy among all the people, which was peculiarly intensified by the shouts of the bondman and the insolvent, because it was the day of the release of the former, and restoration of the property of the latter.

3d. Christmas, the day on which the birth of Christ is celebrated and his nativity recognized, has also been observed for many centuries, since the reign of Dioclesian up to the present, if not before. Christian people and Christian nations every where have made it a day of special honor, nevertheless, thousands regard it as a day of desecration and festive revelry, while others run wild with drunkenness, and honor it with bacchanalian retorts. They treat the birth of Jesus with solemn contempt, and hundreds of church members regard it as a day to shake hands with sin, and compromise with crime.

4th. For the sake of brevity, we will only notice one or two more days which have been honored for certain events that have changed the order of things in the nations history. For ages Catholicism had been the prevailing religion in England, but in consequence of some small opposition in the executive circles of the Government, Catesby, and some other disappointed and desperate hearted Catholics, planned a scheme known as the 'gunpowder plot,' for the murder of the king and the destruction of both houses of parliament. It was resolved that Guy Fawkes, one of the number should set fire to a train of powder which they had prepared; they were all ready, and the 5th, of November 1605, was at hand, the day to which parliament was prorogued. But God averted the horrid catastrophe by its timely discovery, and gave catholicism its death blow, and crowned the protestant faith with eternal honors which ever since has gathered strength with increasing years, till its mighty volume of sacred truths have spanned the broad Atlantic and dashed against American shores—not broken, but divided into religious orders of different faiths—and have swelled our valleys with notes of joy, and dotted our hills with rebounding praises. Thus, the 5th, of November, will ever stand prominent among the days of English commemoration.

5th. The 4th of July is especially familiar to every school boy in this our once cursed, but now blessed country. The white people have made it a day of gratitude and general rejoicing ever since 1776, consequently guns are fired; bells are rung; flags are raised; speeches are delivered, and every mode to express their feelings of pleasure is resorted to, because on that day they threw off the British Yoke, and trampled under foot the septre of despotic tyranny. They raised the standard of independence on that ever memorable day, and every man rallied to its support by the declaration of Independence. An aged sire stood in the steeple of Independence Hall in the city of Philadelphia for hours with the iron tongue of a bell in his hand, shaking his head the while at the assembled multitude, when questioned upon matters relating to his mission. As soon as every name of that august assembly convened within, was appended to that mighty document, which has ever since defied the world, a little boy shouted out 'ring! ring!' and with all the power of a freeman, he struck that bell one hundred blows, (the same number of days it took Abraham Lincoln[1] to smelt out the ball of liberty, from September, 22d, 1862, to January 1st, 1863,) and the bell in response chimed out the irons words engraved upon its rim, 'Proclaim liberty throughout all the land, and to the inhabitants thereof' and thus the stone cut out of the mountain without hands, as seen by the ancient king, made its first revolution towards filling the whole world, as was then predicted, for I hold that America and her Democratic principles and institutions is the great stone which is spoken of by the prophet Daniel. . . .

This great Continent slept in the cradle of undisturbance for thousands of years. God seemed to have held it back for some important purpose, while Asia, Africa and Europe were the world's theatres, and men of all sizes, colors and languages were playing out the drama of life. While nations were rising on the one hand and crumbling on the other. America laid quietly beneath her green bowers and blooming foliage. Her minerals, her exhaustless resources, rested in their beds of silence, and for ages they slept in peace from the hand of enterprise.

---

1. Abraham Lincoln (1809–65) was the sixteenth president of the United States (1861–65).

The Northmen, those mercenary adventurers from Sweden, Denmark, and Norway, came over here five hundred years before the time, but God thwarted their designs, and sent them back, till America should get ripe. The Indian and the roving beasts, true, lived in herds and petty dynasties from the Atlantic to the Pacific Ocean, but they only fed the soil, preparatory to the introduction of enterprise. No gospel messengers went forth to herald the claims of the world's Redeemer, nor summons men to a sense of reason. At length Columbus came, and in his wake ten thousand followed. God removed the obstructions on the one side, and human genius clamored for the world on the other. Settlement and colony succeeded each other, as they ran from the land of fettered conscience, many claiming also a desire to christianize the Indians, the aborigines, of this country. James Oglethorpe,[2] one hundred and thirty years ago, came over with 120 emigrants—his leading idea being to teach the Indian—to this now blood-stained State of Georgia. But he was only a drop in the bucket to the multitudes that came to other parts. God saw this spirit in them and was pleased. The pilgrims to, long before that, had moored the May Flower to the edge of Plymouth Rock, and with knees bent and uplifted hands had consecrated this land to God, and to just and holy ends. The same year—two hundred and forty six years ago—avaricious greed had stolen twenty negroes or sable children from Africa, and a Dutch ship entered the mouth of James river, and landed them at Jamestown in old bone-bleached Virginia, that State where hoarded guilt and hellish crime lie piled to mountain height; that State, like the mother of harlots, who has poisoned by her slave mart (Richmond, the blackest spot on God's earth) all the other States of the South, and finally plunged them into an inextricable vortex, where unbridled vengeance stalked in gigantic strides, and wrote death upon all their institutions of injustice. However, resuming the subject again, this was the introduction of the slave trade, and for many years it was kept up, meeting with the approbation of the most prominent men of the world. The early settlers of this country had run from outrage themselves, and had manifested a desire to civilize the heathen, and to build up an asylum for the oppressed of all nations, and to enact laws which would contemplate justice to all men. Therefore, God seeing the African stood in need of civilization, sanctioned for a while the slave trade—not that it was in harmony with his fundamental laws for one man to rule another, not did God ever

---

2. James Oglethorpe (1696–1785) was a British soldier, member of Parliament, reformer, and founder of the last colony in British America, Georgia.

contemplate that the negro was to be reduced to the status of a vassal, but as a subject for moral and intellectual culture. So God winked, or lided his eye balls at the institution of slavery as a test of the white man's obedience, and elevation of the negro. The extremities of two colors, white and black, were now to meet, and embrace each other, and work out a great problem by the sanction of Heaven for the good of mankind. The African was, I have no doubt, committed to the care of the white man as a trust from God. That he should clear up the land, and pioneer the march of civilization, by agricultural labor and domestic pursuits is a fact about which I have no hesitancy in admitting. That the white man should have made him work and exacted so much daily toil as was commensurate with the necessities of life and the developments of the nation's resources, was all in keeping with order and sense, for he was by virtue of his superior advantages, thereby, his superior in intellect, and the guardian of the negro. But that the white man should bar all the avenues of improvement and hold the Black as he would a horse or a cow; deface the image of God by ignorance, which the black man was the representative of, was the crime which offended Heaven. We gave the white man our labor, yes! every drop of sweat which oozed from our face he claimed as his own. In return, he should have educated us, taught us to read and write at least, and to have seen that Africa was well supplied with missionaries. Their Doctors of Divinity should have told them, that we had rights, and the people must respect them. Had ministers exhausted half the learning and study in showing the white people their duty to the negro as a trust from God, that they have in trying to prove the divine right of slavery, Africa would have been two-thirds civilized to day, and the nation twice as wealthy, and the bones of a million of our countrymen would not now lie bleaching over every Southern State.

The Fourth of July—memorable in the history of our nation as the great day of independence to its countrymen—had no claims upon our sympathies. They made a flag and threw it to the heavens, and bid it float forever; but every star in it was against us; every stripe against us; the red, white and blue was against us; the nation's constitution was against us; yes! every State constitution; every State code; every decision from the supreme court down to the petty magistrate; and worse than all every church was against us; prayer and preaching was against us—enough to make us fall out with God himself. And why was it? We had always been loyal. The first blood spilt in the revolution for the nation's freedom, was that of Crispus Attacks,[3] a full blooded negro. A negro, then, was the pioneer of that liberty which the American people hold so dear. England tried all through the revolutionary war to make us traitors to our country, but failed; we stood firm then and are firm still. Was it then because we were not really human that we have not been recognized as a member of the nation's family? Are we not made as other men? Have we not all the bones, muscles, nerves, veins, organs and functions that other men have? Are there any differences in our women? *White men can answer that question better than us.* And so far as intellect is concerned, are we not as susceptible of improvement as they are? Cannot we learn anything they can? If we cannot, why make it a crime to be found teaching a negro? for it was a penitentiary act in this State, though it was not unlawful to teach a horse to read and write. But the whites not only refused to learn us themselves, but refused to let us learn *at all* if they could prevent it; at least law was against it, which was argument enough. They seem to have forgotten that they were shutting up in darkness, by refusing intellectual development, that immortal spirit; that undying principle; that spark of Deity which was created with exhaustless resources, with a mind, though minute at present, will one day swallow down, or comprehend the mysteries of the universe. Oh! slavery, thou horrid monster! Thy days are numbered! Thou wast a curse to this nation; but far in the distance I hear the last sounds of thy rumbling departure, saying, gone! gone! forever gone! Had the white people treated slavery as a trust from God, it would never have ended in a terrible war. It would have gone on until it became a social burden. It would have passed away so imperceptibly that no one would have felt the shock; more like a weary man going to sleep. But the way it was treated, and the ends to which it was appropriated, was an insult to God. And nothing less than floods of his burning fire and the thunders of his scathing judgment, poured out upon the guilty heads of the violators of this law, and crimsoned acres of ground with the heart's gore of tens of thousands, could satisfy divine justice, and make slavery despicable in the eyes of a country which had loved it so dearly and nurtured it so long. Men, yes—men of every rank and position—had become darkened to the true status of manhood, because worldly gain lay at the bottom of all his moral considerations. . . .

---

3. Crispus Attucks (1723–70) is generally regarded as the first person killed in the Boston Massacre and therefore the first American killed in the American Revolution.

But it is useless to prowl through ancient history to prove our manhood. . . . Unlike the white man—we have no desire to enslave them or deprive them of their oath, disfranchise them, or to expatriate them. All we want is our rights in common with other men, and let them have theirs'. When the nation first called upon the colored men to rally to its flag, a howl and a whine was raised North and South that, 'If you arm the negroes, you can never discipline them; they will be cannibals, kill all the women and children and eat them into the bargain.' But at length the negroes were armed, and Ethiopia stretched for her hands to God with a musket in them. Twelve hundred of us were placed on a bend of the James River, known as Wilson's Landing.[4] Shortly afterwards, Gen. Fitz Hugh Lee[5] came down upon us with twenty-five hundred men. As soon as he drove in our pickets, a flag of truce was sent in to demand a surrender of the place or he would take it, and *death* should be the penalty of our refusal. We however defied his army, so he opened the contest, which raged in fearful suspense for the space of four hours. He charged us three times, and finally left, leaving three hundred dead and wounded on the field. These negro cannibals (for I was one) went out, took up his wounded, carried them to our hospital and treated them kindly. *White man, show a better heart.*

The fact is, we have a better heart than the white people. We want them free and invested with all their rights. We want to treat them kindly and live in friendship; yet, I must say, as I believe, that as soon as old things can be forgotten, or all things become common, that the Southern people will take us by the hand and welcome us to their respect and regard. I look forward to the day when the white people of the South will not exhibit one half the prejudice they do North, for they know us, and we know them; but at present they are peevish, because they think themselves subjugated, while the poorer class never did like us at best. It was also said that the colored people contemplated a cold blooded insurrection during the Christmas holidays,[6] and several of our white friends, I learn, had grave apprehensions about its possibility. I knew then, as I know now, that it was all a piece of nonsensical

---

4. The Battle of Wilson's Wharf, May 24, 1864, took place in Charles City, Virginia, as part of Ulysses Grant's Overland Campaign.

5. Fitzhugh Lee (1835–1905) was a Confederate cavalry general who later served as governor of Virginia (1886–90) and as a US general in the Spanish-American War.

6. See Dan Carter, "The Anatomy of Fear: The Christmas Day Insurrection Scare of 1865," *Journal of Southern History* 42, no. 3 (August 1976): 345–64.

fudge. What have we to insurrect for? Are we not *free* and *eternally free*, and do we not know it? Away with such a hallucination! We never insurrected when we had something to insurrect for.

It was also said, and Southern fanatics rode that hobby everywhere, 'That if you free the negro he will want to marry our daughters and sisters,' that was another foolish dream. What do we want with their daughters and sisters? We have as much beauty as they? Look at our ladies, do you want more beauty than that?

All we ask of the white man is to let our ladies alone, and they need not fear us. The difficulty has heretofore been, *our ladies were not always at our own disposal....*

This is a day of special gratitude to Heaven for many blessings which follow in the exit of slavery.

1st. This is a day of gratitude for the privilege of meeting as other people. Heretofore, we could not meet without being under the supervision of some white man. We were watched, feared and suspicioned. Three colored men could make a threat, and five hundred white men would rush to arms. The whites should thank God with us, for now they can rest quietly, they have no fears of being murdered, nor have they to sit up all night to watch us; no patrol duty to perform; no fears of us running away. They ought to thank God that they are relieved of that burden, and we of our fears—neither party having to watch the other, but all can attend to their own business.

2d. This is a day of gratitude for the general destruction of slavery; for slavery was a reactionary curse. It rebounded back upon the white man, while it degraded the status of the black. This trafficing in human blood, buying and selling, seperating man and wife, parents and children, hardened the hearts and numbed the conscience of the whites and made them cruel and wicked. It petrified their sympathies and deadened their fine sense of justice and made their moral ideas a blank scroll. The result was, they were not near so benevolent in charitable acts as they should have been; consequently, thousands of white children grew up in their midst without any education for the want of free schools. On the other hand, it tended to make us thievish because we regarded it right to filch what we should have had as the reward of our labor. It also tended to make us untruthful, telling lies to escape punishment, or to deceive our owners for some personal comfort which our best men would regard as a necessary prerequisite.

3d. This is a day of gratitude for the freedom of schools. Heretofore, law and rule closed against us books of every description. The Bible, God's eternal WILL and requirements was a sealed book. His pledge, his sacred truths, and all the guarantees of his grace were bared and belted against us by the law of the land. Education the hand maid of religion, God's great articulative organ of communication, hung palsied in the scales of prejudice, or was looked up by the greed of worldly gain. But now the channels of learning are free to all; we only have to launch our vessel and sail in its current to the port of distinction: Our big men, heretofore, were Barbers, Tailors, Bootmakers and Carriage drivers. If we saw John driving our 'Massa and Missus,' O! how we coveted his big position. But now our big men can be Lawyers, Doctors, Editors, Astronomers, Chemists &c.

4th. This is a day of gratitude for the freedom of mind. Heretofore our immeasurable intellects were also enslaved—that is the most damning feature of slavery. But now with a mind, mighty in its resources, though, at present undeveloped we can prowl through Heaven, earth and hell, and claim their extensions as domain of its play. Problems will be made plain, and mysteries will lay bare their long entombed wonders.

5th. This is a day of gratitude for the freedom of matrimony. Formerly there was not security for domestic happiness. Our ladies were insulted and degraded with or without their consent. Our wives were sold, and husbands bought, children were begotten and enslaved by their fathers, we therefore were polygamists by virtue of our condition. But now we can marry and live together till we die, and raise our children and teach them to fear God, O! black age of dissipation, thy days are nearly numbered.

6th. This is a day of gratitude for the freedom of the Gospel. Formerly the Southern ministers were chained or curbed in proclaiming the mandates of Heaven. If one felt disposed to preach the full meaning of the text 'to do to all men as you would have them to do to you,'[7] he trembled, feared, and flaged. The learned men of the world were shut out from the South. You could not preach the pure gospel, nor anyone else[.] God's word had to be frittered smeared and smattered to please the politics of slavery. The key of the Gospel was held by the hand of slavery, but now as slavery is dead and its dungeon opened by Abraham Lincoln the Hercules of freedom, the angel of the cross can fly forever with a free Gospel to all men.

---

7. Matthew 7:12.

7th. This is a day of gratitude for the freedom of labor. Heretofore our chief study was, how to do the least work possible and escape punishment. Labor was not sweetened by reward—it was forced from us. We believed that no man had a right to build fine houses, and revel in pomp and splendor on the sweat of our face, while we dragged out an existence in tattered want and destitution. But now we can work with all the muscle of a freeman. Will you not do it? I believe you will, and now as labor is popular, and it being man's normal position, let us show the world we can perform it.

8th. This is a day of gratitude for the pledge of the nation to the eternal security of all the blessings, and others that I have not time to mention. The nation's great emblem is no longer against us, for we claim the protection of the Stars and Stripes. The glories of its fadeless escutcheon will ever bid us go free. Its mighty forts, guns, and magazines, have Liberty engraved upon their thundering music. The constitution has covenanted with us for mutual protection, it says, 'save me should a foul hand attempt to desecrate my folds, and I will save you from the iron heel of oppression.' . . .

But I must stop, and before doing so, let me say that I have not refered to the cruelty of slavery to incite your passions against the white people. I have done so in order to tell you for what we had reason to thank God and hold this day in special remembrance. To the contrary let us love the whites, and let by-gones be by-gones, neither taunt nor insult them for past grievances, respect them; honor them; work for them; but still let us be men. Let us show them we can be a people, respectable, virtuous, honest, and industrious, and soon their prejudice will melt away, and with God for our father, we will all be brothers.

On the Eligibility of Colored Members to Seats in the Georgia Legislature

Delivered at the Georgia State Legislature, September 3, 1868

SOURCE: Ethel Maude Christler, "Participation of Negroes in the Government of Georgia, 1867–1870" (master's thesis, Atlanta University, 1932), appendix B, https://radar.auctr.edu/islandora/object/cau .td:1932_christler_ethel_m.

In this speech, Turner addressed the attempt by white members of the Georgia legislature to expel thirty African Americans—including Turner—from the House of Representatives.

Mr. Speaker:

Before proceeding to argue this question upon its intrinsic merits, I wish the Members of this House to understand the position that I take. I hold that I am a member of this body. Therefore, sir, I shall neither fawn nor cringe before any party, nor stoop to beg them for my rights. Some of my colored fellow-members, in the course of their remarks, took occasion to appeal to the sympathies of members on the opposite side, and to eulogize their character for magnanimity. It reminds me very much, sir, of slaves begging under the lash. I am here to demand my rights, and to hurl thunderbolts at the men who would dare to cross the threshold of my manhood. There is an old aphorism which says, "Fight the Devil with fire," and if I should observe the rule in this instance, I wish gentlemen to understand that it is but fighting them with their own weapon.

The scene presented in this House, to-day, is one unparalleled in the history of the world. From this day, back to the day when God breathed the breath of life into Adam, no analogy for it can be found. Never, in the history of the world, has a man been arraigned before a body clothed with legislative, judicial or executive functions, charged with the offence of being of a darker hue than his fellow-men. I know that questions have been before the Courts of this country, and of other countries, involving topics not altogether dissimilar to that which is being discussed here to-day. But, sir, never, in all the history of the great nations of this world—never before—has a man been arraigned, charged with an offence committed by the God of Heaven Himself. Cases may be found where men have been deprived of their rights for crimes and misdemeanors; but it has remained for the State of Georgia, in the very heart of the nineteenth century, to call a man before the bar, and there charge him with an act for which he is no more responsible than for the head which he carries upon his shoulders. The Anglo-Saxon race, sir, is a most surprising one. No man has ever been more deceived in that race than I have been for the last three weeks. I was not aware that there was in the character of that race so much cowardice, or so much pusillanimity. The treachery which has been exhibited in it by gentlemen belonging to that race has shaken my confidence in it more than anything that has come under my observation from the day of my birth.

What is the question at issue? Why, sir, this Assembly, to-day, is discussing and deliberating on a matter upon which Angels would tremble to sit in judgment; there is not a Cherubim that sits around God's Eternal Throne, to-day, that would not tremble—even were an order issued by the Supreme God himself—to come down here and sit in judgment on my manhood. Gentlemen may look at this question in whatever light they choose, and with just as much indifference as they may think proper to assume, but I tell you, sir, that this is a question which will not die today. This event shall be remembered by posterity for ages yet to come, and while the sun shall continue to climb the hills of heaven.

Whose Legislature is this? Is it a white man's Legislature, or is it a black man's Legislature? Who voted for a Constitutional Convention, in obedience to the mandate of the Congress of the United States? Who first rallied around the standard of Reconstruction? Who set the ball of loyalty rolling in the State of Georgia? And whose voice was heard on the hills and in the valleys of this State? It was the voice of the brawny-armed negro, with the few humanitarian-hearted white men who came to our assistance. I claim the honor, sir, of having been the instrument of convincing hundreds—yea, thousands—of white men, that to reconstruct under the measures of the United States Congress was the safest and the best course for the interest of the State.

Let us look at some facts in connection with this matter. Did half the white men of Georgia vote for this Legislature? Did not the great bulk of them fight, with all their strength, the Constitution under which we are acting? And did they not fight against the organization of this Legislature? And further, sir, did they not vote against it? Yes, sir! And there are persons in this Legislature, today, who are ready to spit their poison in my face, while they themselves opposed, with all their power, the ratification of this Constitution. They question my right to a seat in this body, to represent the people whose legal votes elected me. This objection, sir, is an unheard of monopoly of power. No analogy can be found for it, except it be the case of a man who should go into my house, take possession of my wife and children, and then tell me to walk out. I stand very much in the position of a criminal before your bar, because I dare to be the exponent of the views of those who sent me here. Or, in other words, we are told that if black men want to speak, they must speak through white trumpets; if black men want their sentiments expressed, they must be adulterated and sent through white messengers, who will quibble, and equivocate, and evade, as rapidly as the pendulum of a clock. If this be not done, then the black men have committed an outrage, and their Representatives must be denied the right to represent their constituents.

The great question, sir, is this: Am I a man? If I am such, I claim the rights of a man. Am I not a man, because I happen to be of a darker hue than honorable gentlemen around me? Let me see whether I am or not. I want to convince the House, today, that I am entitled to my seat here. . . . I assert that by the time you take off the mucous pigment—the color of the skin—you cannot, to save your life, distinguish between the black man and the white. Am I a man? Have I a soul to save, as you have? Am I susceptible of eternal development, as you are? Can I learn all the arts and sciences that you can—has it ever been demonstrated in the history of the world? Have black men ever exhibited bravery, as white men have done? Have they ever been in the professions! Have they not as good articulative organs as you?

. . . There are no two men alike—no two voices alike—no two trees alike. God has weaved and tissued variety and versatility throughout the boundless space of His creation.—Because God saw fit to make some red, and some white, and some black, and some brown, are we to sit here in judgment upon what God has seen fit to do? As well might one play with the thunderbolts of heaven as with that creature that bears God's image—God's photograph. . . .

The negro is here charged with holding office. Why, sir, the negro never wanted office. I recollect that when we wanted candidates for the Constitutional Convention, we went from door to door in the "negro belt," and begged white men to run. Some promised to do so; and yet, on the very day of election, many of them first made known their determination not to comply with their promises. They told black men, everywhere, that they would rather see <u>them</u> run; and it was this encouragement of the white men that induced the colored man to place his name upon the ticket as a candidate for the Convention. In many instances, these white men voted for us. We did not want them, nor ask them, to do it. All we wanted them to do was, to stand still and allow us to walk up to the polls and deposit our ballots. They would not come here themselves, but would insist upon sending us. Ben. Hill told them it was a nigger affair, and advised them to stay away from the polls—a piece of advice which they took very liberal advantage of. If the "niggers" had "office on the brain," it was the white man that put it there—not carpet-baggers, either, nor Yankees, nor scalawags, but the high-bred and dignified Democracy of the South. . . .

. . . If you deny my right—the right of my constituents to have representation here—because it is a "privilege," then, sir, I will show you that I have as many privileges as the whitest man on this floor. If I am not permitted to occupy a seat here, for the purpose of representing my constituents, I want to know how white men can be permitted to do so? How can a white man represent a colored constituency, if a colored man cannot do it? The great argument is: "Oh, we have inherited" this, that and the other. Now, I want gentlemen to come down to cool, common sense. Is the created greater than the Creator? Is man greater than God? It is very strange, if a white man can occupy on this floor <u>a seat created by colored votes</u>, and a black man cannot do it. Why, gentleman, it is the most short-sighted reasoning in the world. A man can see better than that with half an eye; and even if he had no eye at all, he could forge one, as the Cyclops did, or punch one with his finger, which would enable him to see through that.

It is said that Congress never gave us the right to hold office. I want to know, sir, if the Reconstruction measures did not base their action on the ground that no distinction should be made on account of race, color, or previous condition! Was not that the grand fulcrum on which they rested? And did not every reconstructed State have to reconstruct on the idea that no discrimination, in any sense of the term, should be made? There is not a man here who will dare say, "No." If Congress has simply given me merely sufficient civil and political rights to make me a mere political slave for Democrats, or anybody else—giving them the opportunity of jumping on my back, in order to leap into political power—I do not thank Congress for it. Never, so help me, God, shall I be a political slave. I am not now speaking for those colored men who sit with me in this House, nor do I say that they endorse my sentiments, but assisting Mr. Lincoln to take me out of servile slavery, did not intend to put me and my race into <u>political</u> slavery. If they did, let them take away my ballot—I do not want it, and shall not have it. I don't want to be a mere tool of that sort. I have been a slave long enough already....

I stand here today, sir, pleading for ninety thousand black men—voters—of Georgia; and I shall stand and plead the cause of my race until God, in His providence, shall see proper to take me hence. I trust that He will give me strength to stand, and power to accomplish the simple justice that I see for them....

These colored men, who are unable to express themselves with all the clearness, and dignity, and force of rhetorical eloquence, are laughed at in derision by the Democracy of the country. It reminds me very much of the man who looked at himself in a mirror, and, imagining that he was addressing another person, exclaimed: "My God, how ugly you are!" These gentlemen do not consider for a moment the dreadful hardships which these people have endured, and especially those who in any way endeavored to acquire an education. For myself, sir, I was raised in the cotton fields of South Carolina, and, in order to prepare myself for usefulness, as well to myself as to my race, I determined to devote my spare hours to study. When the overseer retired at night to his comfortable couch, I sat and read, and thought, and studied, until I heard him blow his horn in the morning. He frequently told me, with an oath, that if he discovered me attempting to learn, that he would whip me to death, and I have no doubt he would have done so, if he had found an opportunity. I prayed to Almighty God to assist me, and He did, and I thank Him with my whole heart and soul.

Personally, I have the highest regard for the gentleman from Floyd (Mr. Scott),[1] but I need scarcely say that I heartily despise the political sentiments which he holds. I would pledge myself to do this, however: To take the Holy Bible and read it in as many different languages as he will. If _he_ reads it in English, _I_ will do it; if _he_ reads it in Latin, _I_ will do the same; if in Greek, _I_ will read it in that language, too; and if in Hebrew, _I_ will meet _him_, also, there. It can scarcely, then, be upon the plea of ignorance that he would debar me from the exercise of political rights. . . .

So far as I am personally concerned, no man in Georgia has been more conservative than I. "Anything to please the white folks" has been my motto; and so closely have I adhered to that course, that many among my own party have classed me as a Democrat. One of the leaders of the Republican party in Georgia has not been at all favorable to me for some time back, because he believed that I was too "conservative" for a Republican. I can assure you, however, Mr. Speaker, that I have had quite enough, and to spare, of such "conservatism." . . .

But, Mr. Speaker, I do not regard this movement as a thrust at me. It is a thrust at the Bible—a thrust at the God of the Universe, for making a man and not finishing him; it is simply calling the Great Jehovah a fool. Why, sir, though we are not white, we have accomplished much. We have pioneered civilization here; we have built up your country; we have worked in your fields, and garnered your harvests, for two hundred and fifty years! And what do we ask of you in return? Do we ask you for compensation for the sweat our fathers bore for you—for the tears you have caused, and the hearts you have broken, and the lives you have curtailed, and the blood you have spilled? Do we ask retaliation? We ask it not. We are willing to let the dead past bury its dead; but we ask you, now for our RIGHTS. You have all the elements of superiority upon your side you have our money and your own; you have our education and your own; and you have our land and your own, too. We, who number hundreds of thousands in Georgia, including our wives and families, with not a foot of land to call our own—strangers in the land of our birth; without money, without education, without aid, without a roof to cover us while we live, nor sufficient clay to cover us when we die! It is extraordinary that a race such as yours, professing gallantry, and chivalry, and education, and superiority, living in a land where ringing chimes call child and sire to

---

1. Dunlap Scott, who represented Floyd County, Georgia, in 1868.

the church of God—a land where Bibles are read and Gospels truths are spoken, and where courts of justice are presumed to exist; it is extraordinary, I say, that, with all these advantages on your side, you can make wa[r] upon the poor defenseless black man. You know we have no money, no railroads, no telegraphs, no advantages of any sort, and yet all manner of injustice is placed upon us. You know that the black people of this country acknowledge you as their superiors, by virtue of your education and advantages. . . .

You may expel us, gentlemen, but I firmly believe that you will some day repent it. The black man cannot protect a country, if the country doesn't protect him; and if, tomorrow, a war should arise, I would not raise a musket to defend a country where my manhood is denied. The fashionable way in Georgia, when hard work is to be done, is, for the white man to sit at his ease, while the black man does the work; but, sir, I will say this much to the colored men of Georgia, as if I should be killed in this campaign, I may have no opportunity of telling them at any other time: Never lift a finger nor raise a hand in defense of Georgia, unless Georgia acknowledges that you are men, and invests you with the rights pertaining to manhood. Pay your taxes, however, obey all orders from your employers, take good counsel from friends, work faithfully, earn an honest living, and show, by your conduct, that you can be good citizens. . . .

You may expel us, gentlemen, by your votes, today; but, while you do it, remember that there is a just God in Heaven, whose All-Seeing Eye beholds alike the acts of the oppressor and the oppressed, and who, despite the machinations of the wicked, never fails to vindicate the cause of Justice, and the sanctity of His own handiwork.

Speech at National Colored Convention

Delivered at the National Colored Convention, Washington, DC,
January 13, 1869

SOURCE: *Macon American Union*, January 29, 1869

Turner spoke after being named the convention's chair.

Gentlemen of the National Convention:

I do not regard this unexpected honor, so much as a compliment to my personal worth, as a recognition of the constant labors I have endeavored to perform for several years in the cause of equity and justice, and the acknowledgement of the intrinsic worth of my noble constituents in the State of Georgia.

No convention of colored men possessing such an army of talent and literary worth, ever met upon the American continent before. In its composition we have the inestimable pleasure of seeing the Minister, the Lawyer, the Doctor, the Statesman, the Artisan, the Farmer, indeed all the professions are represented, from College Presidents down to the commonest occupation.

To be ungrateful for such an honor would be an unpardonable crime. I shall endeavor to discharge the high duties of my office, as impartially as my abilities will enable me. You, I hope, will recognize the importance of being orderly, and exhibiting that high sense of characteristic dignity, which should always prevail in an intelligent assembly. Gentlemen will remember they are being watched by Congress, and the Nation. Your words are not merely to float off upon the wavy vibrations of the atmosphere, and thus be swallowed up, and lost in oblivion, but they are to be reiterated by the broad mouth of the public press, and weighed in the scales of the public mind.

The cause for which we have met is more than noble; our object is divine, and God will crown it with success, sooner or later. Manhood rights is all we want, South, North, East and West. And it will not be long before the fossilized Democrats of this country, will see humanity recognized and clothed with all its God-given rights, kick and brawl as they may. The sceptre of equity is but the sword of justice. And every man in America must acknowledge it as the mace of God, and Heaven's thunder-bolt hurled against oppression.

Again, thanking you for the honor conferred on me, in being selected to preside over your temporary deliberation, I wish to inquire the further pleasure of the Convention.

A Speech on the Fifteenth Amendment

Delivered in Macon, Georgia, April 19, 1870

Source: Henry McNeal Turner, *Fifteenth Amendment: A Speech on the Benefits Accruing from the Ratification of the Fifteenth Amendment and Its Incorporation into the United States Constitution* (n.p., 1870)

On March 30, 1870, the Fifteenth Amendment officially went into effect, guaranteeing that "the right of citizens of the United States to vote shall not be denied or abridged by the United States or by any State on account of race, color, or previous condition of servitude." Less than three weeks later, Turner was among the many African Americans who rejoiced at what they saw as the solidification of their rights and their assurance of a place in the American fabric.

Fellow Citizens:

I am here to rejoice with you in celebrating one of the grandest events and inestimable blessings that ever crowned a nation's brow or marked the term of a generation; verily this is an eventful dispensation. The drama of national purity and excellence is fast reaching its zenith and culminating in the climax of fadeless glories; the onward stride is marvelous. The purest elements that ever composed the organic structure of a country have been incorporated in ours. This truly is the age of humanitarianism; the triumph of liberal ideas; the march of fraternal feelings and the dying day of domination and conquest.

The devouring lion and the harmless lamb, for the first time, can now repose together under the shades of a republican government. The weakest creature between the shores of the two greatest oceans on earth can slumber peacefully under the benign whispers of that national sovereignty which bids him FEAR NOT.

Nearly one hundred years ago the revolutionary sires laid the foundation of these United States by proclaiming the declaration of Independence in the face of the British tyrant, and cemented the stones with the blood of a thousand battles. This foundation was broadly laid and embodied vast proportions.

It attracted the astonished gaze of mankind because no such a fabric had seen the light of Heaven since the gloom of the Adamic rebellion had shaded the verdant bowers of Eden. But while it was far in advance of any structure then known to mankind, it was still lamentably defective, and incommensurate to the wants of this progressive era of untrammeled intellects and unfettered consciences. Its great arms embraced the sons of every nation, and legalized their heirship, save the darker hued sons of Ham. For what reason they were left out of the category (seemingly for a time by the pleasures of Heaven,) I am not able to explain, unless for the same reason that God hardened Pharaoh's heart: that he might show the sceptics and rationalists of the nineteenth century that he still held the rein of government on earth, and executed his purposes among the armies of the sky.

However that may be, the ratification of the Fifteenth Amendment to the Constitution, all will concede, is the finish of our national fabric; it is the head stone of the world's asylum; the crowning event of the nineteenth century; the brightest glare of glory that ever hung over land or sea. Hereafter, the oppressed children of all countries can find a temple founded upon civil rectitude and religious equity, ample enough to accommodate them all and durable enough to vie with all coming time. . . .

Less than four hundred years ago nothing was known of this continent beyond the visionary dreams of a few geographical speculators. The inexhaustible treasures of the Alleghanies and the rejuvenescent valleys of the Mississippi were slumbering where the foot of the civilized explorer had never trod, awaiting the galvanic shock of enterprise to dismiss their lethargy and whirl them into action. Why Providence permitted this country of boundless resources to lie dormant while Asia, Europe and Africa were the world's theaters, I am inadequate to explain, but for the fact that it was destined to be the greatest theater of all, as has been thus far evinced by its grand career. This isolated country, however, at the proper time was aroused from its slumbers by the electric touch of enterprise. . . . The negro race was first introduced into this country by the contingency of avarice in the year 1620, just two hundred and fifty years ago.

Jamestown, Virginia, was the place of his disembarkation. Here was a human being to all intents and purposes. A being too, who had to play an important part in the dramatic arena of the newly discovered country. But the low order of his previous culture seemed only to fit him for a place between man and beast. Therefore, the status of the negro was rated and fixed in proportion to his pecuniary adaptation. This naturally consigned him to a degraded condition; and while he gave evidence of a higher sphere of importance in his susceptive and rational powers, these powers were interpreted by his after oppressors and construed through the color of greed and force of cupidity to be special endowments by the Creator to enable him the better to grace the relation of a slave. Public sentiment at first, however, adjudged and accorded him the mild protection of a sentient creature, restricted to minors. But as cotton, rice and sugar rose in value as national commodities, these were even lopped off by gradual incursions, till the negro, as a race, became as a prey to the ravenous wolves of all nations. The evidence of his manhood, as evinced by every reasonable instrumentality known in the catalogue of human exploits, gave no protection, afforded no shield, no relief, no bulwark, against the prowess of insatiable avarice. He demonstrated both his manhood and patriotism in religious zeal, in his moral bearing, on the bloody fields of war, amid the thunders of the navy, and the clanking of ten thousand sabers. Wherever the white man went, whatever he did, said, thought or wrote, was imitated by the negro; even the white man's dreams floated through the negro's brains. These attestations of his intellectuality and moral qualities spoke louder in defense of his rights than Senator Sumner could have done with seven thunders uttering his voice. It seemed to be the will of God, however, that we should be goaded and persecuted till a nobler dispensation should dawn. But the murky gloom and dense fog grew more intense till the thobs of freedom's heart had nearly become inert. Thousands wondered if a just being did really rule and reign supreme or was the Bible a fable and the story of the Cross a time-blithing myth. When the yawning gulf of endless servitude would present itself in all the vauntedness of seeming defiance to the powers of earth and heaven. But this was found to be the auspicious time. Verily, the darkest hour is just before day! and what we took to be ill omens, were only the precursors of grand events, big with mercy and ready to break in blessing on our heads. The press had become bitter, sarcastic, wicked and devilish. Politics had become strifish, corrupt and basely prostituted to selfish ends. The Bible was misinterpreted. The pulpit desecrated to a rostrum for the promulgation of wild heresies. God was blasphemously charged with sanctioning human slavery. Sectional broils, personal feuds and local animosities were alienating friends and kindred every day. The halls of legislation were devoted to disgraceful harangues and pugilistic combats. Statesmanship consisted in deceptive pettifoggery— popular topics—in effervescing the diabolical ire of the ignorant rabble, and in leading them to the perpetration of the most horrific deeds ever charged upon mankind since the revel of the bloody orgies. . . .

. . . This brought us to about the year 1860, when Abraham Lincoln, of Illinois, by the grace of God, was elected President of the United States. The policy of Mr. Lincoln had been proclaimed as not favoring the further spread of slavery, but that he would not interfere with its existence in the already slave States. But the slave population was increasing so rapidly that those interested in it were chafed at the idea of the institution being limited to certain bounds, or more extensional confines.

Wherefore, this was considered by the Southern States as the auspicious time to test the right of a State to secede, and thus practicalize their theories; and, in the event of success, they would be enabled to establish a slaveocracy upon an endurable basis, and so perpetuate it for all coming time. South Carolina, the little pestiferous state of my birth and raising, true to her historic instincts, called a Convention and issued a declaration of secession and a manifesto of independence, and inaugurated war by attempting to drive the United States garrison from Fort Sumter; for no sooner did her artillery commence to belch out fire and shell at the National forces, than did the telegraphs flash the rebellious tidings all over the country, and every loyal heart heaved at the fearful news and recoiled at the thought of its inevitable sequence. The gauntlet of a severed country on the one hand and the perpetual establishment of slavery on the other, were then thrown down, and it only remained for the friends of liberty and a model government to take it up. The blast of the war trump was echoed by a proclamation from President Lincoln calling to arms seventy-five thousand soldiers, and suspending the mails in the Southern States. All compromises and pacific blandishments had now fled, and nothing but blood could atone for the errors of the past.

The North and South shortly afterwards met in two serried lines on the bloody fields of Bull Run and made that unknown place ever historic, in a defeat to the Union forces. But this defeat was indispensable, as it told the North, in unmistakable language, what newspapers and periodicals had previously indicated, with no evidence, however, that could convince them: that this was a gigantic rebellion, and in order to crush it out every means and artifice would have to be resorted to known in the genius of civilized warfare. The warning was correspondingly heeded, and resulted in a general uprising in the North, while the South, flush with the glories of a brilliant victory, marshalled her forces and marched them to the front as gallantly as Jupiter even hurled a Vulcan-forged thunderbolt at an evil genius. The contest of blood and carnage was now open, which was destined to crimson acres of land with human gore, and cover hundreds of battle fields with putrescent carcasses and bleaching bones. . . .

A review of that fearful struggle, however, I deem unnecessary, as its details and final result is too well known to thousands who still mourn their departed relatives and friends. Could we but comprehend the significance of many a furrowed cheek, we would see but the channel of rivers and tears which have flowed with saliferous elements down thousands of faces never before saturated from the effects of sorrow or grief. We might read in the gray hairs, hoary heads, wrinkled brows, palid cheeks, broken hearts and untimely graves of thousands, the doleful history of our late war. The end of it finally arrived, however, and lo and behold four million of human beings were found standing in the vale of locomotive freedom, bearing the aspect of creatures who had just been resurrected from the valley of dry bones. A close inspection discovered them to be in a needy condition. True, the negro was free locomotively, but he had none of those indispensable implements of freedom with which to maintain even a povertous existence, he was void of either land, houses, money, education, names or self-sustaining experience. He neither knew how to buy, sell, make, bargain, hire, collect, spend his money, or to tell his name, beyond Dick and Jack, Poll and Sal. I do not enumerate in this account a few city-raised exceptions, but of the negro race through the country and in the aggregate. But there was a need which augmented his indigency and made his condition far more precarious than anything yet mentioned, that was his utter destitution of all civil and political rights. . . .

The first step taken in the erection of the magnificent structure was to amend the United States Constitution, or to change the organic law so as to prohibit slavery and involuntary servitude henceforth and forever. This was to serve as the great fulcrum on which to rest all future levers of whatever name or character, that might be employed in prizing this slave-degraded race up to the exalted status of American citizenship. The amendment was finally ratified after a long and acrimonious scramble; and over twenty millions of American sons and daughters vociferated a grateful shout, and all the civilized world echoes the enrapturing blast, while the minstrelsy of the skies reverberated the tidings in transporting notes. But this did not complete the work; still the smoking embers were there though the building was consumed. The wiry twist of the viper was there, though he had been robbed of his poisonous fangs. The hideous monster lay palsied in death though his frightful ghost haunted the place. Slavery still lingered though under the guise of proscriptive enactment. Its paws were everywhere visible but its weapons were sheathed as an institution. Therefore the contingencies growing out of common life necessitated further legislation; and the sequence was another step—the Freedmen's Bureau Bill. . . .

The next step taken by Congress was the establishment of civil rights, or the adoption of what is known as the Civil Rights Bill. This bill was intended to secure to the negro all the rights known in the range of jurisprudence, and rightly interpreted would have, in my opinion, carried with it every right commonly termed political; but the judiciary construction it received whittled it down to little, if any more than giving evidence in court. And while a regular caravan of *petitmaitre* Judges through the country, unknown to either fame or legal lore, true to their great prototype, Chief Justice Taney,[1] were pronouncing the bill unconstitutional and revolutionary, and the newspapers were gasping and going into death-heaving paroxysms, and their readers falling into appalling convulsions over it, the benefits which actually accrued from it were so worthless that it often reminded me of an old legendary story concerning a mountain being once in great labor merely to give birth to a mouse. The most noisy windmill, strange to say, too, in all the nation against the measure, was Andrew

---

1. Roger Brooke Taney (1777–1864) served as chief justice of the US Supreme Court (1836–64) and was the author of the majority opinion in *Dred Scott v. Sandford* (1857), which declared that African Americans were not and could not be US citizens.

Johnson of Tennessee,[2] who was elected to his exalted position solely upon the assurance of his friendship for the negro. Yet he deserted them and the party which elected him, in a most dastardly and servile manner. But for the treachery of this Tennessee Nero, the public heart would have never been half so poison; and thousands who are dead and sleeping in premature graves would now be living and enjoying the blessings of civil liberty, and augmenting the treasures of our growing Republic. . . .

The reconstruction measures had an analogous bearing on the negro. He was used as the tail of the nation to drag the burdens of taxation and other onerous loads, while fettered by every species of unconscionable restrictions. Had the negro been invested with his sacred and inalienable rights when the almost uncurdled blood of the revolutionary sires were appealing for even-handed justice for all men, and Washington, Jefferson, Adams, and other far-seeing patriots were trembling with fear, at the prospective rupture that slavery was destined to breed in the nation, there would never have been any secession, any Southern Confederacy, any war; nor would the country to-day be groaning under the burdens of taxation, or the oscillations of an unsettled currency. And instead of the country being scarred and disfigured by war arsenals and forts, to-day the rose and magnolia of peace and harmony would be blooming in eternal juviniscents. . . .

. . . The Reconstruction Acts caused such a flutter amongst politicians, and so many technical points, constitutional clauses, legislative acts, and judicial decisions, were hurled at them, that Congress feared, as did thousands, that they might be, after all, a creature of time. Congress also had seen by this time the beneficent working of them; that black men loved the government with all its faults; that untrammeled they would vote for its perpetuity and indivisibility; that they were as grateful for favors as any other people, and consequently must be a people and not monkeys. They had also seen that black men could represent a constituency, fill high positions, and in short, that they possessed all the virtues and vices of white men. These things, and the voices of God and reason, induced them to place this boon beyond the reach of the sacrilegious hand that might one day attempt to wring it from him. Besides, there were several Northern States whose constitutions debarred the negro from voting, notwithstanding the negro had rushed to arms when those

---

2. Andrew Johnson (1808–75) became US president (1865–69) after the assassination of Abraham Lincoln.

States were beleaguered and sacrificed himself upon their flaming altars in defense of their firesides and the green graves of their sires. Thus, step by step the nation strode from January, 1863, when the immortal Lincoln issued his emancipation proclamation, and Hades gaped, the ground trembled, Heaven rejoiced, and ten thousand times ten thousand shouts rent the skies. But there was one thing still needful. This grand superstructure, with its gigantic proportions, intended as a temple for humanity, had gradually rose higher and higher, its foundation was laid in the Thirteenth Amendment, and built up with the stone and cement of the Fourteenth, but the crowning capstone was to be found in something purer still. The Fifteenth Amendment was consequently proposed to the Constitution and received the required sanction of both houses of Congress. The ratification of three-fourths of the States then being necessary to make it a part of that instrument, it was accordingly sent to them, and, I am proud to inform you, that the requisite number gave their adhesion to make it the supreme law of the land. . . . To-day, all honor to Heaven, and thanks to the American people, we stand before the majesty of the law the peers of any other class of citizens. America is redeemed. Our rights have been emancipated as well as our bodies and guaranteed by the breath of God's approval. Our sun is no longer beclouded. Our atmosphere is no longer contaminated by the miasma of proscription. All men, regardless of race, color or previous servitude, can execute their will by the ballot, as lightning does the will of God. Thanks to the American, to the German, to the Irishman, and to every naturalized foreigner who aided in the work. May their lives be happy, may their deaths be precious. . . .

This Amendment is an ensign of our citizenship, the prompter of our patriotism, the bandage that is to blind-fold Justice while his sturdy hands holds the scales and weighs out impartial equity to all, regardless of popular favor or censure. It is the ascending ladder for the obscure and ignoble to rise to glory and renown, the well of living water never to run dry, the glaring pillar of fire in the night of public commotion, and the mantling pillar of cloud by day to repel the scorching rays of wicked prejudice. Hereafter the machinery of our government will be run by the consent of the governed, and its symetrical operations will constitute an axiomatic weapon, for all the oppressed nations on earth to battle with for civil liberty. It is a national guarantee, as fair as the moon, clear as the sun, and terrible as an army with banners. It is the chariot of fire that is to roll us beyond the reach of our persecuting Ahabs and perfidious Jezebels. It is to be the angel in the fiery furnace warding off the burning flames. The golden debris from the high bluffs of this most pre-eminent country of all in the world, shall be washed by the currents of our sweet waters to the low lands of tyrant-ridden nations, to enrich their soil by spreading over them a free alluvium. The Fifteenth Amendment is the shining robe covering in immaculate grandeur the nude and exposed parts of our country, which hitherto made her fragile and vulnerable before enemies. It is the star-decked diadem covering her brow; the interjector of royal blood through every vein. It is the towering spire reaching uppermost of all national virtues, and will be like the pole to the needle, attracting men from every plain and every shore.

Our government to-day is the school-house of the world; here unborn children will come from distant climes to learn civil law and judicial equity, and will return to shake Kingdoms in the face of despots, and trample in the dust tottering thrones, and beat or grind Imperial maces to powder.

The noblest specimens of humanity in all countries were mysteriously planted here, by the husbandman of the Universe, for what purpose remained a mystery for ages. We saw an unparalleled interblending of races and colors here, but its purport was a secret. But having finished our national education and receiving our diploma, in the Fifteenth Amendment, we are now prepared to send blood-kin representatives to all nations, to preach equal rights and commence the work of republicanizing the world. . . .

The sons of Africa, too, can unfettered, untrammeled and unhindered, go to the homes of our forefathers and preach a free religious, civil and political gospel. I know some colored men chafe when they hear an expression about going to Africa. I am sorry I find no term in the vocabulary that will represent them milder than fool; for they are fools. The only reason why Africa is unpopular and ignored by some colored men is because of its unpopularity among the whites. It is the greatest country in natural resources under Heaven. But without reviewing its inexhaustible treasures, and how God is holding them in custody for the civilization of the negro, I merely desire to remark that some of our leading men may blur and slur at Africa till their dooms-day arrives. But God intends for us to carry and spread enlightenment and civilization over that land. They are ours and we are theirs. Religion, morality, economy, policy, utility, expediency, duty, and every other consideration makes it our business. We must, we shall, we will, we ought to do it. . . .

Whatever distinction shall clothe the negro through any future day will be attributed to the workings of the Fifteenth Amendment, and he shall be the lily in the valley and as the rose of Sharon, in the high march of our national splendor. If ever Angels congratulated Saints, I fancy that Gabriel, the Arch Seraph, congratulated our heavenly trio, Columbus, Washington and Lincoln, on the day of its ratification, for the grand result of the Fifteenth Amendment and its concomitant blessings. . . .

In conclusion, let me say, let there be no more hostility between Democrats and Republicans about personal liberty and over human rights; let them bury the bone of contention and shake hands of greeting over the glorious result—a cosmopolitan nation.

Honor to the United States Congress!

Honor to the friends of Liberty!

All honor to the God of Justice!

Resignation as Presiding Elder

Delivered in Savannah, Georgia, January 5, 1872

Source: Mungo M. Ponton, *Life and Times of Henry M. Turner* (Atlanta: Caldwell, 1917), 67–72

Announcing his resignation after six years as presiding elder, Turner recapped his career to that point.

Dear Brethren: I have the honor to ask that I no longer be retained in the arduous duties of Presiding Elder. I am aware that since I have signified a desire to retire from the responsible duties the office involves, grave objections have been made by the brethren to my taking such a step. I hope, however, that these objections will be reconsidered, and that I may be allowed to assume a relation to our Conference less arduous and responsible.

Nine years ago, when our country was in the whirl of revolution and battle strife, and the immortal principles of freedom were in doubtful suspense, I left the pulpit and went to the scene of carnage to throw the weight of my influence and physical power on the side of God and a free country. In this capacity I served both my church and my government to the best of my ability, with what success I will leave to other tongues to tell. I will say, however, I endeavored at all times to discharge my whole duty.

At the end of the rebellion, it was thought by the Chief Executive of the nation [Andrew Johnson] that my services were further needed in the South, in assisting to elevate my recently delivered race; and, being mustered out of service as a United States Chaplain, with my brave and gallant Regiment, I was again reappointed a Chaplain in the Regular Army and sent, by Secretary Stanton,[1] to Georgia to labor in the Freedman's Bureau. Here I landed in the fall of 1865; but shortly after my arrival, I resigned this lucrative position, in consequence of some disrespect shown me on account of my color, on the one hand, and the better to serve my Church on the other.

I immediately entered upon the general organization of the A. M. E. Church in this State. At that time we had only one Church and congregation in Georgia, which was under the pastoral charge of Rev. A. L. Standford—St. Phillip's, Savannah, Georgia. And this is the congregation to which I have reference. Brother Standford was necessarily confined to this special locality, in view of the discordant elements which had to be watched with a vigilant eye—thus leaving almost the entire Empire State of the South to my care and supervision. But the field was ripe for the harvest, though it was large and cumbersome; and without a dollar to start with, I shouldered the responsibilities, and trusting in God for help, went willingly to work.

To recount my labors would necessitate the writing of a volume, which I may do at some future day, but, for the present, it must suffice to say that I have had to pass through blood and fire. No man can imagine what I have had to endure but one who has through it. And no man could have passed through it unless he had, as I have, an iron constitution. I started out with the determination of raising up the grandest Negro Conference in America, but I think we have the largest in the world—certainly America cannot boast of an equal, for we have 189 appointments and 226 members. And as for Church government, we have no superiors for our time and chance. I made it a rule to teach and instill the highest system of Church government known to our connection from the commencement of our organization in the state. This rigid training, as many of you here well remember, caused me often to keep you up all night till day would drive us out of Church the next morning; you know it was nothing unusual for me to have you studying, praying and singing for whole nights in Quarterly Conferences, trying to teach both preachers and their officiary what the law of our Church required, even to

---

1. Edwin McMasters Stanton (1814–69) served as secretary of war under Presidents Lincoln and Johnson (1862–68).

the minutest point. And you need not be reminded of my pulpit labors—you certainly have not forgotten how I had to preach three times every Sabbath and every night in the week, for month after month, and then come out of the pulpit and explain the history, character, purpose and object of our Church, for hours, to satisfy the colored and whites, who would often look at me as if I was a bear or a lion; sometimes just commencing the organization of the Church about twelve or one at night. But why attempt to enter upon a detailed review? Why, in one year alone I traveled over fifteen thousand miles in this State, organizing and planting Churches, and superintending the work, together, and preached and spoke over five hundred times. I have also been accused of recklessly licensing preachers by the cargo, etc., because I had to license such a number. I admit that I did, on several occasions, exercise rather extraordinary powers in this respect, but in no instance where the emergency of the case would not justify such action. I was for a long time Elder, Superintendent and everything else, and sometimes had to make preachers of raw material at a moment's notice. I have licensed preachers while riding on the cars, but I always put you through an examination; sometimes would examine you for three or four hours. And while it is not only gratifying to me to know that some of these arbitrarily licensed preachers are among our most useful and intelligent Presiding Elders, but, what is more gratifying, is that not one of them has been expelled or silenced for any crime whatever. Indeed, my hastily made preachers have been among the most useful.

And my labors have not stopped in the religious sphere; but it is well known to everyone that I have done more work in the political field than any five men in the State, if you will take out Colonel Bryant.[2] I first organized the Republican party in this State, and have worked for its maintenance and perpetuity as no other man in the State has. I have put more men in the field, made more speeches, organized more Union Leagues, political associations, clubs and have written more campaign documents that received larger circulation than any other man in the State. Why, one campaign document I wrote alone was so acceptable that it took four million copies to satisfy the public. And as you are well aware, these labors have not been performed amid sunshine and prosperity. I have been the constant target of Democratic abuse

2. John Emory Bryant (1836–1900) served as a soldier and newspaper editor and worked for the Freedmen's Bureau in Georgia. He was also a member of the Georgia House of Representatives. For more on Bryant, see Ruth Carrie, *Carpetbagger of Conscience: A Biography of John Emory Bryant* (Athens: University of Georgia Press, 1987).

and venom and white Republican jealousy. The newspapers have teemed with all kinds of slander, accusing me of every crime in the catalogue of villainy; I have even been arrested and tried on some of the wildest charges and most groundless accusations ever distilled from the laboratory of hell. Witnesses have been paid as high as four thousand dollars to swear me in the penitentiary; white preachers have sworn that I tried to get up insurrections, etc., a crime punishable with death, and all such deviltry has been resorted to for the purpose of breaking me down,—and with it all they have not hurt a hair of my head, nor even bothered my brain longer than we were going through the farce of an adjudication. I neither replied to their slanders nor sought revenge when it hung upon my option; nor did I even bandy words with the most inveterate and calumnious enemies I had; I invariably let them say their say, and do their do; while they were studying against me, I was studying for the interest of the Church and working for the success of my party, and they would expose their own treachery and lies and leave me to attend to my business, as usual. So that, up to this time, my trials have been a succession of triumphs. I have enemies, as is natural, but, at this time, their tongues are silent, and their missiles are as chaff, while my friends can be counted by hundreds of thousands. And I can boast of being one of the fathers of the mammoth Conference of the A. M. E. Church—an honor I would not exchange for a royal diadem. Thus, having reached the goal of my ambition, I only ask now to be retired from the weighty duties of the past, and given the more humble and more circumscribed sphere of preacher in charge. I am perfectly willing, if the Bishop will consent, to let some of my sons in the Gospel be my Presiding Elder, and I trust I shall be able to honor them as highly as they honor me, for I can say I have yet to be resisted or questioned by a single preacher. And while I shall try to rest more regularly and comfortably in my retired relation, and enjoy life more pleasantly than I have in the last nine years, I shall, nevertheless, endeavor to be equaly as useful to the Church in the literary department, for I purpose to give my future days to the literary work of our grand and growing connection. Since I have been trying to preach the Gospel, I have had the inestimable pleasure of receiving into the Church on probation fourteen thousand three hundred and eighteen persons which I can account for, besides some three or four thousand I cannot give any definite account of. And I would guess, for I am not certain, that I have received during and since the war about sixteen or seventeen thousand full members in the A. M. E. Church, by change of

Church relation—making in all nearly forty thousand souls that I have in some manner been instrumental in bringing to religious liberty; and yet I am not quite thirty-nine years old. Hundreds of these persons have, in all probability, fainted by the way and gone back to the world; but I am, on the other hand, happy to inform you that hundreds have since died in triumph and gone to heaven, while thousands are today pressing their way to a better land, scores among whom are preaching the Gospel. I make no reference to these statistics to have you suppose I am better than other men who have not been thus successful, for I am only a poor, worthless creature, and may yet be a castaway; I only mention these facts to express my profound gratitude to God for His abundant favors which have been bestowed upon one so undeserving. If Bishops Payne[3] and Wayman[4] were here, I would take great pleasure in laying my gratitude at their feet for the support they gave me in the early establishment of this Conference; but, as they are not, I trust Bishop Brown[5] will allow me to tender him my heartfelt thanks for the continued manifestations of respect shown me under his administration—he who has so ably presided over our Conference for the last four years, and done so much to advance and elevate the members of this Conference.

I would say also to the brethren of the Conference: You are now Deacons, Elders, Presiding Elders and many of you are pulpit orators, as now you must bear your own responsibilities and look, in addition to your Bible, Discipline and Bishop, to our Father who art in Heaven for direction and counsel; you are welcome to the benefits of my experience at any time you may wish them. But I trust it will not be in my province to exercise any further control over a single member of the Conference. With those remarks, Bishop and Conference, I again pray to be relieved of my heavy, taxing responsibilities. May the God of grace keep you, is my prayer.

---

3. Daniel Alexander Payne (1811–93) served as bishop of the AME Church (1852–93) and played a major role in shaping the church's direction. He was also the first African American to head a US college, serving as Wilberforce College's president from 1863 to 1877.

4. Alexander Walker Wayman (1821–95) was a bishop of the AME Church (1864–95) and the author of the *Cyclopedia of African Methodism* (Baltimore: Methodist Episcopal Book Depository, 1882).

5. John Mifflin Brown (1817–93) was a bishop in the AME Church and an Underground Railroad leader.

On the Present Duties
and Future Destiny of the Negro Race

Delivered at St. Philip AME Church, Savannah, Georgia,
September 2, 1872

Source: Henry McNeal Turner, *A Speech on the Present Duties and Future Destiny of the Negro Race* (Savannah: Lyceum Association, 1872)

In this optimistic address, Turner argued that the future of African Americans in the United States lay in their own intellectual genius.

. . . As we are called upon to-night to address you on vital issues, and as the young men are the only hope of our race, I beg the privilege of digressing from the already stagnant speculations which so frequently evoke applause, and shall ask permission to blaze out a new, though to some a novel rout, which I hope, however, to make sufficiently clear, to convince others that both expediency and utility demand their consideration. They will be directed in the main to the coming men of my own race. I shall endeavor to convince all present that the prospectus of the negro lies in his own intellectual cabinet. The sweetness of a kiss depends upon the admiration we have for the kissed; the greatness of a people depends upon the admiration they cherish for greatness. It is a quality that is either innate or eternally wanting; it can be excited, aroused, and put in motion, but never substituted. I mean that the negro must climb his own ladder if he ever scales the mount of distinction.

I think I hazard nothing in the assertion that notwithstanding the superficial friendship feigned by many for the negro when some political object is in contemplation where his aid is sought, that the majority of the whites, so far as our state is concerned, have failed to prove themselves the intrinsic and disinterested friend of the negro.

Bombastic gas, grandiloquent words, and flippant tongue sophistry, during a political campaign, is no evidence of genuine friendship. We want facts, attested and sustained by such indubitable attestations as will admit of no doubt, and square, right, practically demonstrated and unconditional philanthropy must constitute the motor nerve in this matter. But without reviewing this subject in detail, as there is none more sensitive, I pass on, with the hope of witnessing an early reformation. I would not have you either to understand that I am speaking of those allied with the Democratic party, absolutely, for I include in this catalogue a regular caravan of dough face Republicans, who have stuck like blood-sucking leeches to the black man in times of political excitement but scorn him in times of peace and quiet.

Their treachery to the negro has nearly ruined this State. Some of them have done more to damn the principles of progress than they could undo in a thousand years. But there are noble exceptions in their ranks, among whom we might enumerate grand and great names, who have expanded their talents and strength in the advocacy of the principles which have been incorporated in the organic law of the land. God has seen this exhibition of perfidy, however, much clearer than we have, and in his own good time his negative will foil the acutest ingenuity of evil designing men. . . .

. . . I trust to present vividly to your minds, the importance of the colored race, observing the morale of an old adage, vulgarly expressed. "Root hog or die," for these sentiments must be our shibboleth before we can realize what Providence has in reservation for us, and it is high time the negro had found out that fact. . . .

The primary duty which lies at the threshold of all other considerations by virtue of it being first in importance, is that of acquiring a liberal education. I do not mean such a superficial knowledge of the letter as will barely enable you to read and write and cipher a little, or a dreamy knowledge of Geography and History, for they are merely the alphabets to an education. But I mean a thorough and practical acquaintance with all the branches of

English literature, and the classic inclusive. Profound thought and polished diction can only be acquired by rigid training, and perfection in them must be obtained by laying the foundation in youth. You will at once perceive that this is the work of our young men, as those among us of advanced years, are too busily engaged with domestic duties to devote to study the time required, if they were ever so susceptible of learning. A mind must be in a passive state to receive the impressions which education is wont to fix upon its tablet, so that the pupil should either be above or below the daily concerns of his bread and meat, by having some one to provide, or being already provided for by wealth. It is well known that our ministry is terribly paralized, and accomplishes but little for the want of that early intellectual training and moral discipline by which alone they can prepare the community to distinguish falsehood from truth; to comprehend the theological tenets of the day; to receive higher and broader views of duty, and to apply general principles to the diversified details of life, which, too, would no longer leave the domestic and practical duties of life the subject of accidental impulse.

A finished education forms the basis of all future success, and the deeper we dive in the limpid truths of reason and philosophy the higher we can rise when we engage our minds in the busy pursuits of life. By this, also, language becomes chaste, perception clear, judgment balanced, and imagination plumes her lofty wings for appalling flights. Our pulpits to-day groan beneath an ignorant ministry, and polished oratory is comparatively a stranger, while professional pursuits are barren among our people. The late revolution left us free, and the 15th amendment has guaranteed the right of citizenship, but we are lamentably wanting in the sphere of professional men, a necessity too fraught with fearful evils to any people. . . .

Another thing deserves more than a passing notice in this connection, that is the want of colored writers. I know of nothing that has worked so much to our disadvantage as our carelessness in this respect. I have been asked a thousand times, why we had no history, and I have both gaped and sighed in giving a reply, so as to make time to fumble with the fingers of my mind, amid the dusty records of the past, trying to scratch up a little, which when collected was too frequently doubtful as to its authenticity. There is no doubt but what we have been too derelict in all ages, about noting events connected with our history. . . .

. . . Another item of history that would be appreciated by unborn millions, would be our fearful contests while passing through the ordeal of

reconstruction. How our newly enfranchised orators mounted the platform, destitute of experience and education, and made the woods, old fields,
churches, barns, horse stables and constitutional conventions ring with the
music of their burning eloquence, while clamoring for equal rights before the
law; yes, some grand son of what is commonly called a dirty, black, ignorant
negro will, through the aid of such a historian, tune his lyre to the music
praise, and hang a bow of glory over the tomb of his grand sire that shall
never fade while the sun shines or stars dance. . . .

I would like to state another thing just here, that is, I have grave doubts
about this being the ultimate home of the colored race any way. I do not
believe we are ever to be expatriated from this country; but I am of the opinion that our people will one day turn their attention to Africa and go to it. I
fear we cannot, for a great while, hold our own against the whites, with their
numerical strength on the one hand and their fearful competition on the
other. Besides the land and the money are theirs, and we are not going to be
satisfied always in the capacity of water-carriers and wood hewers. We must
have railroads, stock in telegraph companies, insurance companies, factories,
&c. This is essential to our growth, up building, and material advancement.
How are we to acquire it? either by going to Africa or out West and settling
on new territory. It is utterly impossible for menial laborers to ever acquire
wealth; one here and one there may overcome the obstacles and rise up a
little, but the masses will go from bad to worse. . . .

Africa holds out the greatest inducements to the colored man of any
other spot on God's green earth; her resources are boundless: her climate
unsurpassed: her minerals incomprehensible: her productive resources amply
sufficient to feed the world ten thousand years, and her temporary ample
enough to give every human being a homestead on the face of the globe,
whose value would defy dollars and cents.

Can any sane man presume for a moment that Providence will allow
these garnered treasures to lie in the bowels of the earth forever. The idea
is preposterous in the extreme. No sir: the time will come when the negro
race will thirst for those climes as the hart does for the water brook, and
omniscient skill will provide the means for his importation. . . .

. . . There is no more abolition hobbies to ride; no more proscriptive laws
to complain of; no wailings to make over Governmental ignorings. We can
no longer charge the white race with obstructing the avenues of knowledge,
and bolting up the word of God; or filtering the Gospel through the seive of

their prejudices, or cauterizing the qualities of virtue.—The nation's decayed tooth has been extracted, and there's no more grim features to distort the countenance. Physical fury have expended itself upon the carcass of slavery and all its concomitant evils, and the huge monster lies paralyzed in death, and the voice of God, and reason now thunders from on high in the pregnant words of the immortal Milton—

Awake! arise! or be forever fallen.

Our orators must now tune their harps for another chant. The words that moved a nation's heart but yesterday will fall dead upon the auditory organ of to-day. The line that divided the South and the North into sectional parties have been washed away by the flood-tides of liberty; the shafts of heaven's vengeance that once plowed the nation, have been entombed by the sons of freedom; and we in common with other American citizens are shielded by the eagis of the law. And if there is anything that may well bestir our pride and evoke mutual congratulations, it is the fact that as a race we, the colored people, are law abiding citizens.... When our newspapers shall condemn the guilty, denounce the wrong, and hurl thunder-bolts at public crimes, be the perpetrators white, black, Republicans or Democrats, a new era will dawn upon us. Heretofore negroes were always guilty, white men always innocent; but the time is coming when merit and demerit will be considered, be the person white or black.

By observing these suggestions, gentlemen of the Lyceum, what do we next behold but a grand and glorious future.—As I look down through the rolling em[b]razures of the coming hereafter, I see the negro raising higher and higher; with manly stride and gallant tread he climbs the hill of fame; he writes his name on the scroll of honor, and dignifies his black skin; he stamps his deeds in legible characters on the rock that was smitten by the rod of liberty; he vindicates his manhood by intellectual achievements, and snatches the honor of his sires from under the tongue of defamation. Educated, polished, wealthy, and refined, he stands in the blaze of future ages, and pours forth his burning eloquence at the bar, while the earth trembles beneath his feet. His flat nose, his kinky hair, his thick lips, and his long heel, will be admired, while from beneath this rude exterior shall shoot forth the incontestable traits of moral purity, and yet grander evidence of an intellectuality that the world cannot and dare not question. The wild gesticulations and the risible idiosyncrasies that now make the negro the funiest creature on earth, whose peculiar habits and mirthful temperament affords amusement for the world one day will be sobered down and brought under the mos[t] sensitive control. White men then will not be driven to the necessity of blacking their faces, redening their lips, and wiging their heads with the kinks of some dead negro's hair, to furnish laughter for the stage and theatre. But if they are not careful he will spell-bind and trance-chain them as completely when he shall thunder from the rostrum and forum as he does now when he dances and cracks jokes on the comedian stage. . . .

Be encouraged ye black sons of America, for there is a better day coming. Already the beacon lights dot the golden shore, and the day-star sheds its meridian splendors.—The chrysalis have been rent by the breath of God, and the caterpillar is throwing off the rugged hull in which he crawled and toiled, it now only remains for him to make a few more struggles, and transmuted into the lovely butterfly he will spread his wings upon the breeze and drink nectar from the sweetest flowers, as he shall bask and luxuriate in the dimless glare of unclouded splendor. His deeds shall be the subject of praise, and his heroism shall be the theme of the poet; the electric spark shall dart from shore to shore, and whisper his massive thoughts and thundering words, while kings shall tremble and empires quake. The future historian shall dip his pen in the azure heavens when he shall sit down to record his history, and dream for words to scan his exploits. . . .

But I have said enough for one lecture; but before concluding allow me to say, gentlemen, that these thoughts may be regarded rather fanciful if not visionary, but do not be deceived, these results will surely be realized, "for God is able out of these stones to raise up children unto Abraham.["][1]

---

1. Matthew 3:9.

The Negro in All Ages

Delivered at the Second Baptist Church, Savannah, Georgia, April 8, 1873

SOURCE: Henry McNeal Turner, *The Negro in All Ages: A Lecture Delivered in the Second Baptist Church of Savannah, Georgia* (Savannah: Patton, 1873)

In this speech, Turner navigated the intersections of race and religion. By adopting a prophetic persona, he refuted much of the science of the day.

LADIES AND GENTLEMEN,

We live in an age of investigation, scrutiny, and moral and intellectual enlightenment. Every question bred in human imagination with all their natural of assumed phases, are passing through the ordeal of the most searching analysis. This might be justly entitled the Laboratory age; for there is nothing in the infinite realm of nature but what is wrestled with by the infinite genius of man, from the most crude and grotesque material, to the most attenuated film or subtilized monad which connect mind and matter, indeed the most etherealized fancies, as well as the cogitative reverie, are made the themes of criticism, and are reduced to the status of speculative philosophy.

The elementary principles of matter, the most intricate and mazy laws of nature, the fossiliferous inscriptive bearing tablets of the hoary past, which have slept in quiet solitude for countless ages, have of late been aroused by the hand of genius, and whirled into marching line by the battle gong of thought.

Theology, science, art, and history, have all received an impulse from the estuary state of the mind. The Stygian river with its seven-fold curls, have been crossed, and the blooming flowers of knowledge are now being plucked. Inquiry seeks a path through the dense forest of an unexplored wilderness, but is foiled in the effort; because the sole of an intellectual foot has never strode this way, but a thousand more enter the arena, with glittering scythes, and level the sward, an highway is thrown up—an avenue extends from the centre to circumference, and the mysteries of ages are brought down to the comprehension of the school-boy, while they scintillate the grandeur of nature and the glory of nature's God.

What the wise savants and bards of old, read in the fickle scintillations of their heated imaginations, have been established and incorporated in the principles of philosophical science, and now course investigation, and defies criticism, the theories of the past, the labyrinthine mysteries of the mythological world, the dread and horror of superstitious fancies, the groundless opinions and wild conjectures that awed the ignorant, and engrossed the minds of philosophers and poets, have been illumined by the sun beams of a brighter era, and stripped of their capricious whims; while truth stands out in bold relief and throws down the gauntlet to her enemies and laughs to scorn her foes.

It confronts alike the superstitious venerable with the undated antiquity, gorgeous with all that refinement and art can do to give them the polish of exquisite perfection, and weave around them illusive charms and magic craft, she assails the vices of the motley rabble in spite of their rancor or numbers, and binds in fetters the sneering Epicureans. The stubborn stoic, the phlegmatic Academician, the logomachical babbler, the pragmatic figure head, and the political time serving weather cock. Truth regards not the opinions of illustrious authorities, nor does she pity the mistaken dupes of false theories, however honest to their conviction the devotees may be. Armed with truth, Paul stood on Mars hill, and thundered at the Areopagus, and challenged the isms of the age, with a determinativeness that neither Socrates or Plato ever dreamed. Martin Luther stood in quiet serenity amid a storm of error, because he wore the mail coat of truth, and shook Germany so severely, that the throne of papacy trembled, and the dark haze of the middle ages rolled away, as if touched by the wand of Omnipotence.

Truth, however, has had to fight its way, inch by inch, and foot by foot, for the forces of error have been large, vigilant, alterative, and unutterably presumptuous, encouraged by innumerable votaries, error with shameless voracity strode in every direction, and with an insatiable greed sought to destroy the last vestige of truth. But like the serpent that licked the file, she only realized her danger when the mouth was tongueless. And strange as it may appear, the struggle has not been confined to mere technicalities, but to self-evident truisms. The forces of error have been marshalled against the most palpable teachings of nature, as ferociously as against the simple revelations of Holy Writ. Led on by that vile foe of earth and heaven, who assaulted Omnipotence upon his throne, and who served hell as an attorney when the humanity of the son of God staggered beneath a forty days fast, it is not a source of surprise that error should be so defiant and blushless, even in the grand blaze of an illuminated age.

The subject of this lecture is, *The Negro in All Ages*. My reason for choosing this theme grows out of a conversation which took place between a white gentleman and a white fool some time since on the Central Rail Road, in my hearing, which you will better understand by the following statement:

After passing Millen, the dinner house on that road, two white men came in the car where I was sitting to take a smoke, they occupied the seat in my rear, I heard one whisper to the other: That's the notorious Turner, who says, the other, the negro Mogul? Yes, was the reply, said the other, I have read his speeches repeatedly, but never saw him before. Well, said one, how do you so count for his ability, intelligence or smartness, or whatever you may call it? For I never can believe that a negro has a soul, he certainly does not belong to the human family, &c. The other gentleman after making a lengthy and able argument in defense of the negro's having a soul, concluded by saying, but you must remember that Turner is not a negro; for he is mixed blooded.

Here I could no longer keep silent, speak I must or die; and whirling my head around as though a ball had struck me on one side, I said, yes, but Dr. Garnett [*sic*][1] of New York is not mixed, neither is Major Delaney[2] of S. C.,

---

1. Henry Highland Garnet (1815–82) was an abolitionist, minister, and orator who in 1865 became the first African American to deliver a speech in the US House of Representatives. See Derrick Spires, "Flights of Fancy: Black Print, Collaboration, and Performances in 'An Address to the Slaves of the United States of America' (Rejected by the National Convention, 1843)," in *The Colored Conventions Movement: Black Organizing in the Nineteenth Century*, ed. P. Gabrielle Foreman, Jim Casey, and Sarah Lynn Patterson (Chapel Hill: University of North Carolina Press, 2021), 125–53.

2. Martin Delany (1812–85) was an abolitionist, journalist, and orator. See Tunde Adeleke, *Martin R. Delany's Civil War and Reconstruction: A Primary Source Reader* (Jackson: University Press of Mississippi, 2020).

mixed, nor is congressman Elliott[3] and Cain[4] of that State mixed; and Turner or you either might sit at any of their feet and learn instructive lessons. Bishop Ward[5] of this State is not mixed; and a man of more natural eloquence and enchanting oratory, does not walk the soil of Georgia. These distinguished gentlemen said I, are all so black, that a white man would be regarded as a fool; who would attempt to claim kin with any of them. But at this juncture, the learned ass that started the conversation, picked up his carcass and conveyed it to another car, and left the other gentleman and me to laugh at his stupidity. But said the remaining gentleman, do you know there are a number of white people in this country who talk in the same way?

Ladies and gentlemen, it will not be my aim this evening, to try to prove that the negro has a soul, but if all white men were as ignorant as the one just referred to, it might be necessary to prove that the whites have one; I shall not question either or attempt to defend the souls of either. A denial of a soul to either race, would be to advertise my own ignorance and insult heaven; and to admit it as a self-evident fact, as it is, would be a useless expenditure of time. The question I propose to deal with, is the negro like other people, and are other people like the negro. Does he belong to the same stock, or in other words, is he an emanation of the same source? I shall assume that he does....

Men for ages have been trying to contemn and ignore the negro race; but in the language of Mr. Crummell,[6] there is hope for Africa yet....A few weeks since, Hon. Frederick Douglass[7] animadverted through his organ severely; upon a paragraph, he saw in one of my speeches in regard to Africa. Wherein I stated, that I did not believe this country would be the ultimate home of the negro race, that I believed our race would one day turn their attention

---

3. Robert B. Elliott (1842–84) was a member of the US House of Representatives from South Carolina (1871–74).

4. Richard H. Cain (1825–87) was a US Representative from South Carolina (1873–75 and 1877–79) who, along with Turner, was elected bishop of the AME Church in 1880.

5. Thomas Marcus Decatur Ward (1823–94) was a bishop of the AME Church (1868–94). He was the first representative of the church to serve on the Pacific Coast.

6. Alexander Crummell (1819–98) was a priest who founded St. Luke's Episcopal Church in Washington, DC, the city's first independent Black Episcopal church, and an early contributor to Pan-African thought. See Wilson Jeremiah Moses, *Alexander Crummell: A Study of Civilization and Discontent* (New York: Oxford University Press, 1989); Alexander Crummell, *Destiny and Race: Selected Writings, 1840–1898*, ed. Wilson Jeremiah Moses (Amherst: University of Massachusetts Press, 1992).

7. Frederick Douglass (1818–95) was an orator, abolitionist, newspaper editor, and social reformer.

to Africa, and go to it. Mr. Douglass accused me of clandestinely aiding the Colonization Society, and hurled his philippics at me in a most frightful manner. Since then, I have given the Colonization scheme some attention; I have read one or two works, which has opened my eyes, and enlarged my store of information, and has enabled me to form an opinion.

And with all the admiration I cherish for that great champion of human rights, I think him wrong in his obstinate and irreconcilable repugnance to that institution; I believe the Colonization Society has done good, is doing good, and will ultimately be adored by unborn millions. Through this very Colonization Society some of the posterity of Mr. Douglass may yet sway a sceptre in that now darkened and despised country, but then enlightened and civilized notion, that will rank their names beside such men as Alexander and Charlemagne, with posterity who are now sleeping in the womb of the future. But for the Colonization Society there would be no communication between here and our Fatherland, and there would be no medium through which to convey the waters of life to that famishing people. Why should we despise Africa because the whites do? Let them despise their own fatherland. Whenever I hear the Irish ridiculing Ireland, the English England, the French France, the Germans Germany, the Italians Italy, and the Spanish Spain, then will I as a descendent of Africa consider the propriety of ridiculing Africa. . . .

O! Africa there is hope for you yet, there are better things in store for thee! These are the days of your small things, "but they are not to be despised";[8] for in the pregnant words of the poet:

"There is a light in the window for thee, brother,
There is a light in the window for thee."[9] . . .

I think I hear the voice of God and reason say: Hold! hold!! hold your peace, enough has been said! The negro is a human being, the negro has capacities susceptible of eternal evolutions—he too, is a man bearing the undoubted impress of his maker. And to those monomaniacs, who would rob him of manhood—seek to defame his name—and eclipse his glory I now leave to the wormwood and the gall, and hell must chant their dreadful requiem, and finish the sad story, for I have no organ that can give utterance to the rest.

---

8. Zechariah 4:10

9. Edward Weldon Dunbar, "A Light in the Window," 1858, https://hymnary.org/text/theres_a_light_in_the_window_for_thee_br.

Eulogy of Charles Sumner

Delivered at St. Philip AME Church, Savannah, Georgia, March 18, 1874

SOURCE: Henry McNeal Turner and J. M. Simms, *Memorial Services: Tribute to the Hon. Charles Sumner* (Savannah: Patton, 1874), 10–18

Charles Sumner (1811–74) was a US senator from Massachusetts who opposed slavery and supported Reconstruction. As in this eulogy, Turner often called Sumner the "unquestionable father of civil rights."

My friends, we meet to-day to commemorate and mourn the loss of one of the greatest Americans ever born and nurtured upon our world-famed soil, our grief at the loss of Hon. Charles Sumner finds no expression in words, no relief in tears, and no comfort in the sighs of millions.

A statesman who stood head and shoulders above any of his day and generation. A scholar who had no superior in legal lore or moral ethics. A philanthropist whose capacious affections and great heart encircled the children of every race, clime, and nationality. A citizen whose character was untarnished, a reformer who stood as a watch tower in the van-guard of a revolutionary host. A gentleman who culture, refinement and urbanity blended with an aristocratic demeanor, singularly constituting him a model among equals. An orator whose chaste diction and flowery eloquence will be the emmulation of coming generations.

A hero whose war weapons were bloodless missiles, but terribly invincible, and fearfully destructive on the field of combat.

A philosopher whose analytical acumen comprehended every phase of human character, and sifted the deeds of kingdoms.

A beacon whose flambeau lit up the path of progress and civilization.

A cosmopolitan who had no bounds to his generosity and would have rather been the benefactor of a hottentot than the companion of a prince— but to be short, one of the noblest specimens of humanity of any age, in the history of the world, fell in death from the apex of glory when all that was mortal of Chas. Sumner died.

About twenty-three years ago, a tall, spare looking man, crowned with a majestic brow, and presenting the aspects of great natural ability and the highest acquirable attainments, walked into the senate of the United States, possibly to the consternation of many, and after taking the oath of office, sat down in the midst of those he was destined to eclipse both in glory and renown in a few years. In close proximity sat Samuel [*sic*] P. Chase[1] and John P. Hale.[2] This trio then constituted the only free soil exponents in the Senate. They were the nucleonic forces of those fearful issues which were in a short time to change the land-marks of our country, and baptize the nation with freedom. Up to this time the right of petition was partially denied if it involved the subject of human rights, and those in the Senate who dared to present them were classed among fanatics, agitators, and the most inimical foes the country had.

But for one to so far forget his calling as to attack the wrongs of slavery, was to make himself such an unnatural piece of hybrid monstrosity, that no vocabulary could furnish a name with which to entitle him.

The reputation of Mr. Sumner, though small at that time, had nevertheless, acquired sufficient celebrity to indicate his future course in the Senate; therefore, to thwart any mischievous designs on his part to the special institution whose advocates were always exceedingly sensitive, the pro-slavery senators resorted to every conceivable parliamentary strategy to prevent him getting the floor; but in due time he obtained it, and from the day he delivered his maiden speech to the day of his death he was the grand master of the Senate Chamber.

---

1. Salmon P. Chase (1808–73) was a US senator from Ohio (1849–55), secretary of the treasury (1861–64), and chief justice of the US Supreme Court (1864–73).

2. John Parker Hale (1806–73) was a US senator from New Hampshire (1847–53 and 1855–65).

In a conversation with Chief-Justice Chase in Washington city in 1869, he told me when only three of them were in the Senate (meaning three Abolitionists) they were pointed out and looked at as wild beasts in a cage, but, said he, "Sumner kept them all busy."

For three quarters of a century the Congress of the United States had never had a fearless champion of liberty. True there had been men there who had assumed timid positions favoring free speech, colonization, &c., but there had never been a man there who took bold grounds in favor of a free country. . . .

When Mr. Sumner was called from the ranks of the private citizen to the Senate without having to serve an apprenticeship in the lower house of Congress, or in the executive chair of his State, any one familiar with the history of nations and kingdoms might have known it was portentous of a gathering action.

True, the friends of liberty had able representatives in the persons of Mr. Hale and the late Chief Justice of the United States, but they lacked the dash, the vim, the snap, the dare, the popular defiance, and sledge hammer and battle axe ability, and power, commensurate to the emergency of battle, though great men as they undoubtedly were. But in Mr. Sumner all these characteristics and qualities happily blended, and made him the match of all the learned sophists, of all the time serving political weather-cocks, of all the batten mouth braggarts and bombastic blusterers, of all the wiry tongue rhetoricians and pseudo-logicians, that this or any other country could produce, of all the fabricated fiction, or labyrinthine mazes with which the sharpers of tyranny could festoon their theories. Too noble to do wrong, too great to be mean, too wise to make a blunder, too high to countenance a low act, too solid to be a trickster[,] too pure to be a politician, too just to be partial, too brave to cower before men or devils, too spotless to be slandered in the most calumnious age the world ever witnessed, armed with the helmet of right, and panoplied with a code of principles, as irreversible as the flowing current of the Mississippi river, he stood out as grand and as majestic before the world as thundering Sinai did, when the shuddering hosts of Israel trembled at its base. A vital amazement, an intellectual prodigy, a human creature with superhuman traits, such was Sumner, the man of destiny, molded out of the matrix of heaven by the command of God, to front the reformatory measures born in the middle of the nineteenth century, and well did he do the work assigned. What staggered Hale and disheartened Chase, only fired the soul of the great Sumner.

The Southern statesmen for years had swayed a sceptre of political power over this country, till in many respects they regarded themselves as lords of the manor, but in Mr. Sumner they had an antagonist they were unable to cope with in learning or baffle in argument. But South Carolina the pestiferous State of my nativity, was so bent upon silencing his otherwise impregnable batteries, that she resorted to the bludgeon in the hands of Preston S. Brooks.[3] The sequence was, that in May, 1856, Mr Sumner was knocked down in the Senate Chamber, drenched in his own blood, and the skull that enclosed the finest brain in the world was fractured for life, but this was only the harbinger of greater results. While Mr. Sumner was for a short time silent from the brutal effects of a cowardly assault upon his person, the silence was counter-balanced by the thunders of a hundred volcanoes, which spit forth angry fire, smoke, and seething lava in terrible ebulitions to the consternation of every like ruffian, for the whole North was mad, and even the South was mantled in shame and had to censure her own hero.

But the blood of the saints are said to be the seed of the Church, and so it was in this case, the blood of Mr. Sumner proved to be the seed of liberty, for although he so far recovered as to be able to resume his seat in that body, when he returned, he went with a feeble constitution, but a stronger will and a greater soul, where both he and the blood he shed so profusely, plead the cause of the oppressed. From that time till the overthrow of slavery, Mr. Sumner spoke to man but his blood spoke to God, Mr. Sumner cried to earth but his blood cried to Heaven, Mr. Sumner plead in the Senate but his blood pleas in the skies.

Mr. Sumner with his solid reason and thrilling eloquence touched the hearts of millions, but his blood touched the heart of God, Mr. Sumner marshalled the armies of the nation against the institution of slavery, but his blood marshalled the armies of heaven.

The trio of so-called fanatics above referred to, Sumner, Chase and Hale, could not have made the impression in years with the most learned and

---

3. Preston Brooks (1819–57) was a member of the US House of Representatives from South Carolina (1853–57). A strong proponent of slavery and states' rights, he nearly beat Sumner to death with a cane on May 22, 1856, after Sumner delivered an antislavery speech, "The Crime against Kansas," on the Senate floor. See Joanne B. Freeman, *The Field of Blood: Violence in Congress and the Road to Civil War* (New York: Picador/Farrar, Straus and Giroux, 2019).

elaborate arguments that was made in a day after Sumner fell by the fatal-aimed blow of a ruffian, and wallowed in his own blood.

Mr. Sumner was no politician, he was every whit a statesman; like Webster, he was an orator, but unlike Webster he was inflexible; like Everet[4] he was a philosopher, learned and sagacious; but unlike Everet, he was an impartial philanthropist, with a heart as wide as immensity. Like Clay, he knew what would serve the people as a temporary panacea, but unlike Clay he made no compromises. Like Calhoun he ransacked the dusty records of ages to glean the assembled wisdom of the world; but unlike Calhoun, he used his knowledge to help the poor, needy, and oppressed, and not to perpetuate a vicious aristocracy at the expense of others of the same blood, and none the better by race. Like Bacon,[5] he reasoned on transcendental theories, to aid the cause of justice and refute the wild heresies of his day; but unlike Bacon, he carried a spotless record of the tomb. Like Fox,[6] he was censured for his course by the same power that gave him elevation; but unlike Fox, Massachusetts bowed at his feet and begged pardon.

He was too great to be a politician, for he had no policy, he was as far above political wire-pulling and intrigue, as the heavens are above earth. And yet he was the master politician of the age, because his policy was even handed right. Yes, square right between man and man, founded on the golden rule which was manufactured in heaven,

"Do unto to others, as ye would them do to you."

Nor would I have you to understand Mr. Sumner to be some later day, spawn or plastic fungus, who like a mushroom, sprang up, and under the afflatus of a constituency, adopted a popular course merely for the sake of office; to the contrary, I have the most masterly argument ever delivered in this country; made by him long before he ever thought of the Senate,

---

4. Probably Edward Everett (1794–1865), well-known orator and president of Harvard University (1846–48). Everett also served as a US representative, senator, and secretary of state and as governor of Massachusetts.

5. Francis Bacon (1561–1626) was an English philosopher known as the father of empiricism. He also served as the country's attorney general and lord chancellor.

6. Charles James Fox (1749–1806) was a great British orator.

which he made in favor of mixed schools.[7] It was really he who opened
the schools of Massachusetts to the indiscriminate use of the colored, and
broke down the walls of distinction. At that time, too, he was in the flush
vigor of a young man, and no position assumed could have been more
odious and unprospective. Thus showing, beyond doubt, that he never did
cater to public sentiment, if that sentiment was vitiated and contrary to
the rule of right.

And while he was a friend of all men, a world-wide benefactor, a cosmopolitan in the fullest sense of the term, with inclinations and predilections
as impartial as the sun-beams, which fall indiscriminately upon all races and
climes. He would, nevertheless, seem to be the special friend of the colored
race; yet, he was no more our friend than he would have been of the Jew, the
Irishman, the German, the Italian, or the Frenchman, had they been in our
condition. Jesus said when he was on earth, "I came not to call the righteous,
but sinners to repentance."[8] And again, he said, the whole need not a physi-
cian but they that are sick.[9] Mr. Sumner did not feel that white men needed
his help like the poor negro whose mouths were locked and whose hands
were tied, yet, his great abilities were not by any means restricted to our race,
for when the nation stood in need of one to champion her cause, measure
arms with the diplomats of the world, and vindicate her honor with foreign
powers, to whom did she look but to C[h]arles Sumner? the man who could
read and translate the languages of all civilized nations on the globe, the man
who understood all treaties, all the international laws and the man above all
others in America, who was respected by the great men of every civilized
nation in the world.

The truth is, Mr. Sumner hated slavery, because he thought it was wrong
per se, and subversive of the end, for which his country had been released
from British tyranny[.] White slavery or black slavery were equally obnoxious
to him, and on the other hand he believed as both revelation and reason
teaches, that the negro was the image of God set in ebony, and in a fair race

---

7. In 1849, Sumner delivered a speech before the Massachusetts Supreme Court that was
subsequently published as *Equality before the Law: Unconstitutionality of Separate Colored
Schools in Massachusetts: Argument of Charles Sumner, Esq., before the Supreme Court of
Massachusetts, in the Case of Sarah C. Roberts vs. the City of Boston, December 4, 1849*
(Washington, DC: Rives and Bailey, 1870).

8. Luke 5:32.

9. Luke 5:31.

would win distinction as well as other people. He did not believe in crippling a man and condemning him for being lame, therefore he said give the negro fair play and then if he fails condemn him, but not hamstring you and then ridicule your inactivity.

Such is an epitome of the creed of that great statesman, however, as he saw the colored race the most needy, he gave us the most assistance, for he was in deed and in truth OUR HERO—OUR CHAMPION.

And while we can name a host of true friends—friends who have been tried and found steadfast and immovable, none more so than his colleague for many years, Vice-President Wilson,[10] I do not know of any who could measure arms with Mr. Sumner. He began at home in Massachusetts, and although he found no actual slaves there when he mounted the arena of manhood; he found the cold hand of discrimination, and fought till he had driven it out.

When he went to Washington, he found it the abode of slaves and the den of oppression; he mustered the armies of Jehovah and flayed the monster, for like Hercules he held the poison-fanged viper by the neck till the horrid reptile twitched in death.

He fired the hearts of the North on the one side, and of the South on the other, and opened a chasm which could never close till the negro passed through it on his way to Canaan. He, in conjunction with Thadeus Stevens,[11] Horace Greely[12] and others, held the rod over the great Lincoln, and whipped him step by step and from corner to corner during the late bloody war, till he issued his world-renowned proclamation of emancipation.

At the end of the war, he with Chief Justice Chase and Thadeus Stevens at his side, led the crusade against the admission of the South to representation, till the negro had his oath in the court house, and was clothed with the ballot. These being obtained, he turned his attention to the district of Columbia, and crushed out all distinctions between races and colors so completely that anyone visiting the national capitol to-day, would be astonished to learn that such a hydra-headed monster ever stalked at large in that beautiful city.

---

10. Henry Wilson (1812–75) served as US vice president (1873–75).

11. Thadeus Stevens (1792–1868) was a member of the US House of Representatives from Pennsylvania (1859–68).

12. Horace Greeley (1811–72) was the founder and editor of the *New York Tribune* and a member of the US House of Representatives (1848–49).

When President Johnson sent General Grant,[13] who was no statesman or politician at the time, through the South on a tour of inspection, and he (General Grant) returned and reported things all quiet and peaceable between the whites and blacks, it was Mr. Sumner who rose up in the Senate and told the country that the report was white-washed, and so counterbalanced or counteracted the effects of the report as to turn the tide of popular sentiment in favor of those who stood in need of the protection of the general Government. But on no subject did Mr. Sumner display the majesty of a statesman, and dwell in such convincing power as he did on giving the negro the ballot. Here he showed the resources of his exhaustless intellect as no other statesman living did or could. He challenged the world—he met our foes from every clime and of every dialect, he rebutted their objections by quotations from the reformers of all nations, he made the moralists, the poets, the theologians, the jurists, the scientists, and the axiomatics of every age and clime contribute to this object. He could spare blood to wash the Senate of the United States, and brain-force to deluge the world with ideas. True, he never led a party, but he led the nation—he was greater than a party, besides he lived too far in advance of his contemporaries to lead a party, however noble its aims and commendable its cause; but like a pilot boat he found the channel for the ship of State, and dragged her after him with a slow but a sure glide.

Mr. Sumner had no personal relations he could not sever when they stood in the way of duty, for he would fight his personal friends as hard when he thought them wrong as he would his bitterest foes. Nor did he couch before either power or popularity, he cared no more for a President than for a peasant, if he thought them wrong, duty first and friendship second was his motto. He pinched President Johnson so during his treacherous administration that on one occasion the President got tight, and named him personally in a drunken carousal from the steps of the White House. He even frightened President Grant so about San Domingo[14] that he has been afraid to mention the name since.

---

13. Ulysses S. Grant (1822–85) was a US Civil War general and the US president (1869–77).

14. During his first term in office (1869–73), President Ulysses S. Grant proposed annexing the Dominican Republic, located on the island of San Domingo (now Hispaniola). Sumner opposed the idea and helped to defeat the plan in the Senate. See Dennis R. Hidalgo, "Charles Sumner and the Annexation of the Dominican Republic," *Itinerario* 21, no. 2 (July 1997): 51–65.

Mr. Sumner was not only a man of the finest theories, but he gave practicalization to all his professions. He professed to be a humanitarian, and he carried it out to the very letter. While he lived in the most superb splendor, in a mansion in which there was nothing wanting in the range of human conception, yet that mansion was as free to the blackest negro as to an English Lord.

While his high polish and great refinement made him an aristocrat in the eyes of the masses, yet he felt as much gratification in taking a black man by the arm and perambulating the streets, as he would to be in the train of royal pomp. A few years ago, when on a visit to Washington with Mr. Simms,[15] . . . we had an occasion to visit one of the public buildings in company with Mr. Sumner; and to my astonishment the greatest statesman the sun ever shone upon, walked up between us and locked our arms, and proceeded through the streets and buildings as unconcernedly as if had been in company with his senatorial colleagues; he thought no more of asking a black man to dine at his table, than he did of the whitest man on earth.

Mr. Sumner did not live for himself either, he lived to be a blessing to the poor and needy. The last time I saw his majestic brow and stately person was last spring in Washington, at which time I called upon him to pay my respects as I usually did; our conversation soon turned upon the fight, he waged against the President. I told him, that I like thousands of other colored men in the country; loved him but could not endorse his rabid fight on the President, though I did not doubt, but the President had faults. Well, he said, "that was natural; but if my attack upon the President does no other good, it will drive him to stand by colored people more firmly, to prove that my predictions were false. But said he, a great many of his pap-fed supporters think they have killed me off, but I am perfectly willing to go down, if the colored people can go up, for I am only living for them now; and I can only hope to see the labors of my life crowned with the passage of the civil rights' bill, then and not till then, can I feel that the cause for which so much blood have been shed is complete." . . .

How Christ-like these words, how full of righteousness Mr. Sumner felt years ago, that he was to be one of the chief instruments in the hands of

---

15. James Meriles Simms (1823–1912) was a preacher, editor, politician, and author who was elected to the Georgia House of Representatives in 1868. He and other African Americans who had won posts in the state's government were soon expelled from their positions but were reinstated by congressional order in 1870.

God, of crowning this nation with the diadem of justice. In a conversation between him and myself and several others, who called upon him in 1863, he remarked, "that my blood kindled this fire, (meaning the war,) and when it needed recruiting, John Brown[16] gave his to rekindle it, and it will be utterly impossible now to extinguish it with compromises." A great many northern papers at that time was advocating the policy of offering some overtures to the South, and ending further destruction of life on the battle field. But the last humanitarian act, for which the distinguished Senator labored with such indefatigable devotion, as to merit the praise, the love, the honor, and admiration of our race forever, was in trying to secure the passage of the Civil Rights' Bill, and thus abolish all distinctions between races, colors and nationalities, as well as to give his country what few, if any, upon the face of the globe can claim, a code of cosmopolitan laws. In this the great senator rises to a grandeur that will enshrine his name in the affections of men of every clime. Generations now sleeping in the womb of the future, will come forth with richer words and swifter pens to fringe his name with glittering gems.

When the kings and queens of earth shall be forgotten or remembered in contempt, and the heroes of the battlefield shall no longer be admired, the name of Sumner shall still glow upon the pages of history; and the poet-muse shall weave it into song, while the reformers of all nations will quote his remarks as the preachers of the gospel quote from the sacred scriptures. The only shadow that fell over the dying couch of Mr. Sumner, was the black prejudiced, which had stayed the passage of that bill; for this he had labored for years and waited with patience. I have no doubt but his bludgeon-fractured head and worn-out frame would have died a year sooner, had that bill been passed. It made the soul linger in the body and loth to quit its hold. He would rise up from a bed of prostration and crawl to the Senate Chamber, to watch his Civil Rights' Bill. The desire of seeing that bill become a law was a greater stimulant to his shattered constitution than all the medical excitives known to pharmacology, for he was the unquestionable father of civil rights; it was never thought of till he raised the question. He had even then to educate both colors to its importance and worth. Many colored people at first thought such a measure premature and useless, and, I am sorry to say, I was one.

---

16. John Brown (1800–1859) was an abolitionist, minister, and freedom fighter. He was hanged after leading an 1859 raid on the US arsenal at Harpers Ferry, Virginia (now West Virginia), that he hoped would spark a slave revolt across the South.

For I never could understand the necessity and indispensability of such a measure being enacted, till I read it in Mr. Sumner's speeches. In this God made him the school-master of the nation. Thus he comprehended the wants of the negro better than thousands of them did for themselves, and the wants of the country better than any statesman, living or dead, nor did this knowledge or desire desert him even in his dying hour; the aim of his life became the charm of his death. There stood George T. Downing,[17] the President of our Civil Rights Associations for the United States, a man, too, of culture, taste, and ability, in the name of his race, to minister to the physical wants of our departing hero. Mr. Sumner looked through Mr. Downing as an astronomer does his telescope, and saw behind him five million of his race suffering under the effects of civil proscription; and the hero of civil rights then cast his dying eyes to Mr. Hoar[18] and said, "Do NOT LET THE CIVIL RIGHTS BILL FAIL." Again his life sinks down beneath the turbid waters of death, and all seems still and quiet, for his pulse has refused to beat; but once more he surges to the top, and whispers from the very jaws of death, "Do NOT FORGET THE BILL." And again he sinks, to rise no more forever.

And thus, ends the career of the greatest statesman living or dead; dead did I say? O heavens can it be, Charles Sumner dead?—how cold that word,—is the great Sumner gone?—shall we see his majestic form no more?—is his voice hushed forever?—have we lost our best friend, (God excepted?)—who can fill his place?—shall we ever see it filled?—no, no, no, for the world can only produce one Charles Sumner in a dispensation, never, never will we look upon his like again. O God, but for thee, I should despair to-day and say let me go too[.] But I trust his mantle will fall on some of his compeers, and that another shall lead the measures he inaugurated to a full and complete consummation. Congress can only honor him by the passage of his bill, any memorial services in Congress that does not involve the passage of his civil rights bill, will be a farce, a fizzle and a dishonor of the sacred name of Charles Sumner.

Among the great men of the world, we reckon the names of Cicero, Cæsar, Socrates, Charlemagne, Cromwell, Hamden, Tell, Bonaparte, Burke, Pitt, Fox, Washington, Tousant, Louverture, Webster, Brougham, and a host of other statesmen, reformers, poets, philosophers, scientists, inventors and

---

17. George T. Downing (1819–1903) was an abolitionist and prominent member of the Colored Conventions movement.

18. George Frisbie Hoar (1826–1904) was a member of the US House of Representatives (1869–77) and US Senate (1877–1904).

benefactors. But high above them all we may hang the name of Hon. Charles Sumner, whose spotless life, whose industrious record, whose great abilities, whose triumphant career, and whose heaven-born principles will only be written when the lightening holds the pen and the azure heavens unrolls the scroll of immensity. Farewell thou fallen hero,—farewell to thy noble heart,—farewell Charles Sumner.

Report of the Committee on Resolutions

Delivered at the Georgia Convention of Colored Men, Augusta,
October 8, 1875

SOURCE: *New Orleans Weekly Louisianian*, October 30, 1875

*In the summer of 1875, African Americans in Georgia's Johnson County were
accused of planning an insurrection, and the ringleaders of the alleged plot
faced trial in September of that year. When most of the men were acquitted,
white residents of the area attacked members of the African American community. A few weeks later, Turner and other members of the Georgia Convention
of Colored Men issued a resolution denouncing the charges against the men
and the white response to their acquittal.*[1]

WHEREAS, On or about the 20th of August, a report was raised that the
colored people of Middle Georgia were banding together for the purpose of
inaugurating war upon the whites, and instituting a barbarous and servile
insurrection for the extermination of the same; and

Whereas, It has been charged and published to the world, that the so-
called insurrectionists not only contemplated the perpetration of deeds of

---

1. For more on the "Johnson County Insurrection of 1875," see Gregory Mixon, *Show
Thyself a Man: Georgia State Troops, Colored, 1865–1905* (Gainesville: University Press of
Florida, 2016), chapter 2.

rapine and horror upon the white men and property of the State, but sought the lives of the helpless women and innocent children, a crime which is not only in violation of law, a disgrace to civilization, but one at which a savage might shudder; and

Whereas, It was charged that we, the colored people, desired to assassinate and murder the whites, for the purpose of taking their lands, mules, houses, and other property; and that we had already organized and commenced the pillage and plunder; and

Whereas, Such a charge was never made against us in the days of slavery, when we were subjected to every species of inhuman treatment, and torn from our parents, wives, and children, and all that we had dear on earth, and when we had it in our power to lay the State in ashes with the torch and match and to scatter death and destruction broadcast through the land, and send the shafts of horror with starvation and appall to every door; and

Whereas, The insurrection charged upon the colored people has not resulted in killing, or maiming, bruising, or attempting to perpetrate any violence or harm upon a solitary white individual, male or female, nor in finding in the possession of the colored people any arms or weapons which could be construed into an intention to commit violence; and

Whereas, The letters and papers said to have been found, which revealed the plot of an insurrection, bore upon their face such indubitable evidence of forgery and perjury, that the prosecution dared not present them in the court, at the late trial; and

Whereas, There was not a first class white person in any way connected with raising the report, or appeared upon the witness stand, or even gave credence to the rumor, showing that whole affair emanated from the scullion whites who manufactured the same to gain notoriety and vent their spleen against the colored race, being incapable of rising above a mean act; and

Whereas, The following persons have been murdered, viz: Robert Troop, Morris Troop, Rev. Counsel Oliver, of Laurens county, and Rev. Washington Scott of Burke, and the two men found dead in a pound in Washington county; and other outrages too numerous to mention, such as shooting, whipping, clubbing, stabbing, etc.

Resolved, That we, in convention assembled, representing the various sections of the State, and more especially the portion where the so-called insurrection is said to have existed, *deny the charge in toto*, and brand the false and malicious rumor as a public slander, fabricated and heralded abroad by a set of wicked and mischievous parties to frighten the women, arouse the passions of the whites, and the better to enable them to expend their diabolical hate in murderous assaults upon the colored race.

Resolved, That we unequivocally protest against the persecution to which many of our brethren have been lately subjected in Washington, Johnson, Burke, and other counties, in Middle Georgia, under the false and malicious charge of an attempt to incite an insurrection, when there never has been one justifiable reason to suspect it.

Resolved, That the imprisonment of seventy-nine colored men in the county of Washington and over two hundred in other adjacent counties, when it has appeared by legal investigation (our enemies being in the main judges) that there was no excuse for holding any for trial, was an offense against liberty, justice and humanity, and merits the condemnation of the whole country and civilized world.

Resolved, That while we overlook those of our white citizens who were excited by false rumors and reports, to resentment and enmity towards our innocent brethren, we demand of them as an atonement for this grievous wrong that they detect, expose, and punish the wicked authors of those reports and their principal abettors.

Resolved, That the persecution of which we complain, formed a part of a nefarious conspiracy against the lives and reputation of colored citizens, which was to affect its objects by forgery, perjury and murder under the forms of law, and since it has been happily defeated, we call upon the Governor of this State to show as much energy and zeal in bringing these conspirators to justice as he showed against their intended victims. Otherwise, we shall take it for granted that he was *particeps criminis* to the fiendish plot.

Resolved, That we join in the praise that has been bestowed upon his Honor, Herschel V. Johnson[2] for the ability and impartiality with which he presided in the late trial in Washington and Johnson counties, and thank the jurors who rendered a righteous verdict of acquittal, but we regret that simple justice in a judge, and integrity in jurors where colored men are concerned, are deemed so extraordinary as to call for special admiration.

Resolved, That colored citizens have the same right, as other citizens, to drills, parades, processions, uniforms, arms, societies open and secret,

---

2. Herschel Vespasian Johnson (1812–80) served as governor of Georgia (1853–57), a Confederate senator (1863–65), and a US circuit court judge (1873–80).

public meetings, opinions, and free discussions upon all subjects, and that any attempt by the whites to abridge or prevent these rights and privileges is a violation of law, an outrage upon our liberties contrary to the constitution of our State and of the United States. And further, we declare before God and the world, that we will not be deprived of them, and to their maintenance we pledge our lives and honors.

Resolved, That neither the past nor present disposition of the colored citizens of Georgia, as a body justifies those who charge us with wanting in the duties of citizenship. We are in favor of order, quiet, and industry. We expect, and always have, to get land or other property only by buying it with the accumulations from our toil; we desire peace with our white neighbors, on the basis of equal rights, and mutual respect. When they employ us we expect to give good work, as the crops in the past prove we have given, and we in turn want living wages. We wish to cooperate with them for the welfare of our State and country.

And we demand nothing but a realization in practice of what is theoretically given us by law.

Resolved, That candor compels us to say, that we regard the charge of insurrection coming from parties who inaugurated one of the most *fearful insurrections* known to the nineteenth century, and from whose crimson hands the blood of thousands are still dripping, with very ill grace. And we are led to believe that the phantoms of their own folly must be haunting them yet; otherwise, they would hardly charge the same crime, upon a race which has ever been loyal to their State and nation, and which has no bloody record to tarnish their memories. And we would recommend to them our example.

Resolved, That in the event the Governor and constituted authorities of the State, fail to arrest, expose, and punish the true conspirators, the assassins and murderers of the colored people in Burke, Washington, Johnson and such other counties, as the late disturbances occurred in; that we advise every colored person, male and female to leave the said counties, and move to some other counties in the State or out of the State if necessary. We however recommend them to wait two or three months to see what action will be taken to give protection to life and person.

Genesis 16:13: *"Thou God Seest Me"*

Delivered at St. James' Tabernacle, Savannah, Georgia, November 28, 1875

Source: *Savannah Colored Tribune*, December 4, 1875

Preaching on Genesis 16:13, "Thou God Seest Me," Turner reminds the congregation that God is very present and sees all.

The words of my text, as you all see, are inscribed upon the front of our pulpit, and they seem to be highly appropriate for our consideration, upon our first attempt to speak a word for our Maker after the consecration of this edifice.

"Thou God seest me." These words were uttered by Hagar, the handmaid of Sarah, the wife of Abraham, while she was a fugitive in the wilderness trying to escape from the jealous displeasure of Sarah. You are likely too well acquainted with the narrative for me to expend your time in reviewing it; should there be any who are not, however, I would recommend them to read and study this chapter, as it very aptly pictures God's dealings with us in a manner too significant to ever be forgotten afterward.

In this age of skepticism, and what is worse, pantheism—all Godism, if you choose—when men are trying to overturn the truth of revelation, and make the Bible a myth, and the religion of the ages a mere passion of fanaticism or superstitious frenzy, we cannot examine this question too closely. The times are evil, and doctrines are put forth incessantly, fraught with danger though

robed in the finest fabric of . . . religious philosophy. "Thou God seest me."
That there is a God, that He is omnipresent, almighty, and possesses those
qualities accorded to Him by protestant Christianity. . . . In this sacred edifice,
and upon that presumption, we proceed to notice—

1st. *That God is everywhere present and no where absent.* Says the Psalmist:
"Whither shall I go from Thy spirit, or whither shall I flee from Thy presence.
If I ascend up into the heaven, Thou are there, if I make my bed in hell, behold
Thou art there."[1] Again, "if I say surely the darkness shall cover me, yea the
darkness hideth not from Thee, but the night shineth as the day. The darkness
and the light are both alike to Thee."[2] That God the sovereign of the universe
fills all space and comprehends all the conditions of His creatures, would, it
appears to me, only be questioned by those who cannot reason: yet there are
many people in this world who were born and raised under christian influence, that dared to do it. Their theory is that things move on by a fortuitous
concourse of circumstances, with no definite or centralized power, but that
men are under a watchful and protecting providence from the cradles to the
graves, is too evident for discussion at this day; were it not so what a doleful
state of existence would life be. Think for a moment my friends of being in
a world of so much adversity, misfortune and crime as this, and no arm to
lean upon. . . . Let us think of the injustice we are too frequently subjected
to: the porsecutions we have to endure, and the poverty that many have to
encounter, and of all the disappointments and ills this life is heir to; and yet
no friend, no watching eye, no loving heart caring for us. . . . Hagar's God
watched over her in the wilderness, with her eyes turned toward heaven and
her heart overflowing with joy, she exclaimed—"Thou God seest me." It is
the same God that saw Moses at the foot of Horeb, the Israelites in Egypt,
Daniel in the lion den, Paul and Silas in prison, Luther in his tatters and all
who have been delivered from their sorrows and degradation. Yes, His sleep-
less eye scans from the tall archangel to the sparrow, down to the creeping
insect. He saw the world of mankind groaning beneath the tyrant tread of
Satan and his hellish crew, and gave Jesus Christ His only son to ransom us
from his power, and through His blood to make us the sons of God.

2d. God is acquainted with all our actions and motives. Men see but
a small part of what we do and hear but a small part of what we say. But

---

1. Psalm 139:7–8.
2. Psalm 139:11–12.

God looks into the deep secrets of the heart and the motives that prompt them. Well says the Psalmist, "Thou hast set our iniquities before Thee, our secret sins in the light of Thy countenance."[3] One of the prophets exclaims, "For the Lord is a God of knowledge, and by him actions are weighed.[4] He sees our conduct from our beginning to our end; He numbers the hairs of our heads.

What solemn awe these declarations should produce! How useful should we live! And yet, how careless do we live. What a host of people throughout this city are frittering away their precious moments, this very morning, who ought to be at the church of God. If there is one evil that is more detestable than another, certainly it is the crime of willfully wasting the Sabbath day. I look upon a man or woman who neglects the church, who spends their Sabbaths sleeping, babbling and lounging around, but an inch above a brute. I care not how rich a man may be, how well educated, literally, he is, nevertheless, wanting in thorough civilization, the most that can be said for him is that he is a semi-barbarian. I never neglected to go to church once every Sabbath, when I used to curse and swear. This very moment I venture to say there are ten thousand people in Savannah at no church at all and there is not a colored church in this city half filled. But God sees them—wrath is coming—hell is moving—and in a very short time the reward of their hands will be given unto them. Oh, my friends, think and tremble, hear it and quake.

3d. . . . God sees and takes cognizance of our behaviour: that he hears our words, watches us on the highway, sees us in the family circle, inspects us when buying and selling all notes, frauds, all falsehoods, all evasions, prevarications, and everything that is unholy. And that on the other hand, He sees and fully comprehends the strength of our faith, patience, self-denials, religious zeal and all that builds up christian character.

4th. People are too much disposed to look upon God as being far off, in the mighty distance and not as ever-present in his immediate power. What a mistake they make. It is just to the contrary. Of all things He is the nearest; nearer than you mother, nearer than your wife, nearer than your husband; yes, nearer than the shoes on your feet and the hat upon your head. . . . "Thou God seest me," me individually, not my nation, my State, my city, my

---

3. Psalm 90:8.
4. 1 Samuel 2:3.

neighborhood, my family circle, but me as a personal entity. Take this text home with you. Study and digest it, and do not forget it, and you who disregard the law of morality, weigh these words, and remember that this God who sees you will soon judge you at His bar, that He will be judge, jury and witness combined. Oh, that heaven may sanctify these remarks for eternal salvation is my prayer.

Jeremiah 28:16: "This Year Thou Shalt Die"

Delivered at St. James' Tabernacle, Savannah, Georgia, January 2, 1876

SOURCE: *Savannah Colored Tribune*, March 11, 1876

Turner delivers a sermon that reminds the congregation that death is a reality that one should face and be prepared for.

"This year thou shalt die"—Jeremiah, xxviii: 16. The decree has gone out from God that all men shall die. It may therefore be said, that death is the common lot of man, and yet, no truism has taxed Almighty wisdom more than this, to force its recognition among the inhabitants of the earth. Everybody gives a vague assent to death, yet how few realize the magnitude of that assent. The great bulk of humanity only entertain dreamy ideas of it. Ask a man if he does not know he has to die and he will tell you yes, but its practical effects seldom if ever, enters his mind; he has been accustomed to hearing it said, everybody must die, and he yields a kind of traditional concession without one in ten thousand times thinking of what he is saying, while at the very moment he is speaking death is undermining his constitutionality and the golden moments of life are flying away in swift succession, for

"Death rides in every breeze
And lurks in every flower."[1]

The words of my text is the sentence of God against Hananiah, a false prophet, who, in the days Zedekiah, king of Judah, endeavored to mislead the chosen people of God by lies, and even dared to contend with Jeremiah, the prophet. Hananiah withstood Jeremiah, the prophet, and publicly prophesied in the temple that within two years Jeconiah and all his fellow captives, with the vessels of the Lords house, which Nebuchadnezzar had taken to Babylon, should be brought back to Jerusalem, an indication that treacherous negotiations were already secretly open with Pharaoh—Hophra. He corroborated his prophecy by taking the yoke from the neck of Jeremiah, a yoke he wore by divine command to symbolize the subjection of Judea and the neighboring countries to the Babylonian empire and breaking it. But Jeremiah was ordered to tell the prophetic impostor, that for the wooden yoke which he had broken, iron yokes should be made and substituted, so firm was the dominion of Babylon destined to be for seventy years. This rebuke was accompanied by a prediction of Hananiah's death, which took place in two months after it was made. This false prophet unconditionally promised prosperity to an abandoned and unrepentant generation, and did not so much as exhort them to a reformation. It was just such abominable trash as some men call the pure gospel in this day. All encouragement, promise, privilege, cheer, and hallelujah, without the least warning, discrimination of character, exhortation, or precept. There are preachers in the land by scores, who had rather deliver a fantastic sermon, coined out of an ignorant imagination, and raise a shout, than to utter the sober word of truth and have God's endorsement—time servers and men pleasers were never made to hear the message of heaven. One "Thus saith the Lord," is of more value than a thousand whimsical fancies. Man needs truth, stripped of all its caprices, however severe or terrific it may be.

"This year thou shalt die." was the appalling message which froze the heart of the rebellious prophet. And if we could but part the veil of the future and look through a few weeks or months of the near hereafter we might find ourselves in awful agony too. This is the first Sabbath of the new year—the second day of the year—we have started out to contend with 1876, the great

---

1. Reginald Heber, "Death Rides on Every Passing Breeze," https://hymnary.org/text/ death_rides_on_every_passing_breeze.

centennial year. The whole nation is jubilant, the expectation of millions are high and gleeful. How many anticipations cluster around the future of thousands, yes, tens of thousands, who will never realize them, for God has said: "This year thou shalt die." It may be me, it may [be] you, but be sure it will be some of us, possibly several of us, for all of us cannot weather the storms of life another twelve months. Rev. Daniel Watts, the celebrated blind preacher, told us this morning from this pulpit, that it would be a wonder to himself should he live to enjoy the first Sabbath in another year—we all might say the same. But for the special care that God takes of us, we might write despair upon our every brow. I believe there are a thousand chances to die where there is one to live. Not that death in itself is natural—death is unnatural, abnormal, man was not made to die but to live; his probation should have terminated with an ecstatic transmutation like Enoch and Elijah; no blighting frost should have withered his brow or horrified his change of worlds. But sin gave birth to death, and death, like a hungry vulture, eventually eats us up. His greed is insatiable, his avarice knows no bounds; in search of his prey he darts swifter than lightning, his circuit is from pole to pole, the world is his slaughter house and the earth his cemetery. Millions and billions have fell beneath his stroke, and still the world of mankind is startled at the dread exclaim, "This year thou shalt die!" What a host of us too, will never see a new years Sabbath again. Let us see if we can adumbrate the multitude that will be gone twelve months from today. It is estimated that seventy persons die every minute; then four thousand two hundred die every hour, over a hundred thousand every day, seven thousand every week, three million and twenty four thousand every month; but oh! my God, listen at this, will you? Thirty-six million, seven hundred and forty-two thousand die every year; a multitude too great for the human mind to span. There is not a man on earth, who could conceive of what such a concourse of men and women would be. They would reach in single file, twenty one thousand miles, three feet apart—almost around the globe; and at arms length, they would belt the entire world, and the same number could belt it two or three times at speaking distance. Yet such is the number that must die this year. And should we be visited with the Asiatic cholera, or some other fearful epidemic, this number may be greatly augmented; or suppose we should be visited with such earthquakes, or volcanic eruptions, as have swept tens of thousands away in the twinkling of an eye? For these dreadful calamities may happen at any time. Look how Herculaneum, Pompeii, and Stabiae were flooded with burning lava, and destroyed thousands in one fearful blast.

Look how quick two hundred and fifty thousand perished at Antioch in 526. Think of the terrible destruction that came upon Lisbon in 1755, when in six minutes sixty thousand men and women as good as we are were numbered with the dead. Think of the total destruction of Euphemia, a city in Calabria, where five thousand were swallowed up in a moment, leaving nothing to mark the place but a dismal lake. Think of the volcanic eruptions at Jorullo in Mexico in 1759, when ten miles of level earth were dashed up five hundred feet, burying everything in its ruins. Think of Skaptar Jokul in 1783 which poured forth two streams of burning lava, one sixty miles long and twelve wide, and the other forty miles long and seven wide, and both averging a hundred feet thick. Again, around a mountain in Java in 1772, forty villages reposed in peace, but the mountain sank, carrying the cities and inhabitants with it, leaving a lake fifteen miles long and six broad. . . . Is there any reason we should not be visited with similar judgments? Are we miserable rebels against God any better than those sinners? May not the same judgment come upon some of our cities?—such as New York, Washington City, and God-defying and heaven-daring Savannah, a large majority of the inhabitants of which seem to think of but little else than picnics, ball rooms and blaspheming around grog-shops.

Oh, my friends, pause, pause a moment, the mandate of the eternal is, "This year thou shalt die." Could we but see the streams of tears death will wring from our eyes this year, or hear the screams, groans and lamentations death will exhort before next new year, we would all exclaim, "woe is me." But let me tell these husbands, some of you will follow your wives to the grave this year; wives some of you will weep over your coffined husbands and children before next New Year's day[.] God only knows who it will be, and well it is for us that God does only know, for if we knew it would paralyze the nations of earth and palsy the energies of the world; ships would stop sailing, railroad cars would stop running, commerce would go down, business would be stagnant, stores would be closed, fields would grow up in grass and weeds, while the early victims of death would become frantic with despair; and a wail unlike any since the world began, would be heard through the land, weeping for ourselves and weeping for one another. But while we may all not die this year; it is our every duty to keep a look out for death and prepare for it—life is uncertain death certain. Take this text home with you, write it upon your mantle-piece, post it upon the walls of your house and keep it, before you. Oh that God may save us, is my prayer.

Nomination Speech for James G. Blaine

Delivered at the Republican National Convention, Cincinnati,
June 15, 1876

SOURCE: *Official Proceedings of the National Republican Conventions of 1868, 1872, 1876, and 1880* (Minneapolis: Johnson, 1903), 296–97.

At the 1876 Republican National Convention, Turner was asked to second the presidential nomination of Maine's James G. Blaine (1830–93). Blaine, who had served as a member of the US House of Representatives (1863–76) and as Speaker of the House (1869–75), ultimately lost the nomination to Rutherford B. Hayes, who went on to defeat Democrat Samuel J. Tilden in November. Blaine became a US senator (1876–81) and served two terms as secretary of state (March–December 1881 and 1889–92).

Mr. President and Gentlemen of the Convention: . . . When I left my home in Georgia I went eastward, and determined, in passing through several of the states, to ascertain the will of the people. I knew it would be almost impossible to give Georgia's electoral vote to any Republican, notwithstanding the dead have been raised. Everywhere I went, everywhere I mingled with the people, the name of Blaine seemed to be talismanic. It extorted a cheer, and the people seemed to be alive at the very announcement of it. I rise to-day to second the nomination of James G. Blaine, of Maine. And in doing this, Mr.

President and gentlemen of the convention, I want it understood that some of the names that have been mentioned I revere with a reverence that my tongue cannot express. The name of Morton,[1] the champion of Gov. Pinchback,[2] the defender of the outraged people of Louisiana! I would borrow a Raphael's pen, and dip it in the sunlight of heaven, and write on Morton's brow,— "Honor, eternal honor." But, Mr. President, I believe that we have before us now a name that will arouse the people of this great country in a remarkable manner that the name of Morton cannot. I have nothing to say against Mr. Bristow.[3] I listened to the eloquence of the great poet (!) of New York,[4] as he defended the name of Bristow; and I paid equal deference to that learned son of Massachusetts, our minister to England (!).[5] But, Mr. President, in the person of James G. Blaine we have a Republican about whom there is no question. He commenced with the party, and for twenty-five years he has been in its front, and to-day he stands the champion of Republican principles, I believe, in the United States of America. He gave his own state,—so says an aged and learned doctor of divinity of Maine—to that party, and forever, I expect, buried Democracy on that sacred soil. It will never lift its head there again, I trust. He originated the spirit of the fourteenth amendment. He stood by the immortal Lincoln during the great struggle this country was passing through for freedom and justice and equality to all mankind and to chase out of this nation a set of insurgents who lifted impious hands against that flag that still floats over us, thank God. Mr. President, there is one thing I like about Mr. Blaine: he is a representative of Young America. He is no dead fossil. He is not tied on to any old constitutional barriers that shut out a parcel, a class, of God's humanity, and tie him to a set of principles that are antiquated. One thing more I wish to say of Mr. Blaine, and—I have a dozen points to make, but will make but one now—it is this: But for Mr. Blaine you

---

1. Levi P. Morton (1824–1920) served as the US vice president (1889–93).

2. Pinckney Benton Stewart Pinchback (1837–1921) was a publisher and a Union army officer. He became the first African American elected to a governorship when he won Louisiana's top office in 1872.

3. Benjamin Bristow (1832–96) served as US solicitor general (1870–72) and secretary of the treasury (1874–76).

4. Possibly George William Curtis (1824–92), a well-known white writer and speaker who supported African American equality and civil rights.

5. Possibly Charles Francis Adams (1807–86), the son of President John Quincy Adams and grandson of President John Adams, who served as the US minister to England from 1861 to 1868 and played an important role in keeping the British government from formally recognizing the Confederate States of America.

would have no Republican party to-day. Wait, and I will show it. When the Democrats carried this country, at the last election, the Republican party of those days all over this land was thunderstruck, paralyzed, dead, and bleeding. It was Blaine, standing on the floor of congress, who shook aloft the banner of the Republican party, united the party, and defied the Democracy of this nation, and breathed again the spirit of activity and hope into this prostrate Republican party. Who can deny it?

Consecration Speech of the Azor

Delivered at White Point Garden, Charleston, South Carolina, March 21, 1878

SOURCE: *Charleston News and Courier*, March 22, 1878

Speaking in front of a crowd estimated at five thousand, Turner offered bless-ings and support for a ship, the Azor, *that would carry emigrants from the United States to Africa.*

Fellow kinsmen, we are gathered to celebrate one of the greatest events in the history of this country. The object of this assemblage is to consecrate to the service and care of God this vessel, which is about to cross the trackless ocean. It is not only to bear to Africa a certain number of her sable sons and daughters; it is not only to bear a road of humanity, but to take back the culture, education, and religion acquired here. The work inaugurated then will never stop until the blaze of truth should glitter over the whole broad African continent. Much has been said against this enterprise by croakers and sneerers. It has been so with every great enterprise the world ever saw. In the pages of history, they would find that these habitual fault finders were dead and forgotten—hidden behind the curtain of the past—while those whom they envied and criticized lived and destined to live forever.

The ship stands as a monument to the genius, manhood, and love of race of the Negro, and silences his calumniators who said that he could do nothing. This proved that something could be done, and grander results await in the future. The Negro was an anomaly among nations. He was the only one who had imbibed enough of the prejudices of those among whom he lived to despise and deny his own race. Every other people were proud of its nationality but the Negro, but God had so created him that his dark skin and kinky hair bound him forever to his native country and race, and he could not prevent it. The Negro claimed an American citizenship. Well, in one sense he was an American citizen in so much as he had watered the land with his sweat, purchased it with his blood, and was made of its dust. But he was bound to Africa by dissoluble ties. Here too, the Negro was a race of bootblacks and hostlers and house servants—a nation of menials. Before he could gain his proper position, he had to become his own master and only his own servant, and he had to go somewhere out of the country to do it.

The name "Azor" is a Hebrew word, meaning to aid or be aided. It is beautifully appropriate for she is going to aid those who need aid. To the detractors of our own race, they could present no logic against the civilization of two hundred million of their people—blood of their blood and bone of their bone. The central location of Africa, I believe, was the first land created and the Garden of Eden, and it was intended someday to lighten the world.

Emigration of the Colored People of the United States

Prepared for the National Conference of Colored Men, Nashville, Tennessee, May 6, 1879

Source: Henry McNeal Turner, *Emigration of the Colored People of the United States: Is it Expedient? If So, Where To?* (Nashville, TN: Publication Department AME Church, 1879)

In this address, Turner argued in favor of Black emigration to Africa.

... Much has been said in contravention to the colonization or emigration of the colored people from the United States, not only to Africa, but to any place whatever, except to the horse stable or cook kitchen of the white man. The theory of the maligners of this measure has invariably been that the colored people are to the manor born, and, as such, are citizens of the United States; and anyone proposing a change of locality has been censured in immeasurable terms. Strange as it may appear, too, these denunciators have rarely presented an argument in opposition to colonization to which you could apply one rule of the most distorted logic. As a rule they do not want either reason, analogy, precedent, example, or a scintilla of probability. They simply want the carp of the cynic, and the billingsgate of the profane. I so judge because they have rarely employed anything else in support of their opposition.

The main object against which the contemners of colonization, however, have leveled their shafts of vengeance, has been the American Colonization Society. The traducers of the measure have uniformly screened themselves behind the antecedents of a few rabid slaveholders, who had done some ugly thing, or made some fanatical remark, yet were supporters of this society....

It is not essential to the purpose in view, however, that I should exhaust the time allotted me in an argumentative defense of the Colonization Society. Its record is before us, and sober reflection will ultimately tell its own story infinitely better than any analysis I may be able to give the subject in a few brief moments. I repeat that my purpose is higher than a mere defense of any one society or corporate organization.

This question at issue is, Should the colored people of this country give any support, countenance or sanctions to African emigration? Despite its contemners and host of animadverters, I affirm they should; that it is a grave and an honorable question, meriting the highest considerations as well as the most favorable investigation, viewed from any aspect whatever. I do not propose to present any arguments, based upon logical deductions, to establish their right of emigration there: their freedom presupposes that right. But the question is, Is it right or even expedient? Are there any features about it commendable? I so believe, and to that point I now propose for a few moments to address myself.

1st. We are the descendants of Africa, and as such have no more cause to abhor the land of our fathers than other races have had. And yet I challenge an instance, since, the dawn of creation, where a people have ridiculed the land of their fathers to the same extent as the American negro. He has a detestation to Africa, too, not from choice or a knowledge of any of its objectionable features, but from a prejudicial white rabble, who knew no more about its resources, its wealth and its sanitary advantages than idiots. They contemned the negro in all other respects—his color, his hair, his mouth, nose, lips, heel, language, manner and laugh, and to coronate their scorn and obloquy, they contemn his country.

And we, in our folly, have united with this vicious and garbage-box cavalcade, whereas, if our father land was a desert plain, it ill became us to join in with its defamers; I have heard colored men absolutely charge God with such folly, in their ignorant representations of Africa, that to me it sounded like blasphemy. If it was as hideous as they describe it, no sane man could conclude other than that God was a monster for creating such a place, yet these profaners in some instances knew no more of geography than a man in the moon; they were merely trying to amplify the utterances of some venomous hearted and ignorant headed white maniacs, who were either ventilating their negro-hating spleen, or trying to subserve the purposes of slavery. . . .

2d. Many object to Africa upon the plea of its rumored fatality, that everybody going there prematurely dies. I shall not attempt to refute this falsehood by statistical arguments; it would consume too much time. I will reply by saying the mortality in no part of Africa, neither in Liberia or elsewhere, has ever been anything like that which attended the early settlers at Plymouth Rock, Jamestown, Annapolis, Charleston, Savannah, New Orleans and even Louisville, Ky. . . .

Liberia to-day is no sicklier than the suburbs of some of our own cities, and has never been heir to such dreadful epidemics and inexplicable plagues as have prevailed in several southern cities in the United States; and all reports to the contrary are false alarms.

But let Liberia be ever so sickly. Liberia is not Africa. Liberia is but a speck upon the face of that unexplored continent. Africa is vastly larger than North America, or North and South America together, and the negro there can rear a nation that shall have a wider territory and a larger population by far. From New York to San Francisco is three thousand miles, but from Liberia across the continent is over four thousand.

3d. The right of a people to emigrate to any country is vested in the inducements offered. Now does emigration to Africa offer any? I assert it does.

In this country, although it is our unquestionable home, we are prescribed from Maine to California; but we are too familiar with that fact and its disagreeable sequences to rehearse them here: to catalogue them, would call for the pen of infamy and the ink of hemlock and bitter gall.

But I contend that this proscription is not the result of color so much as of our poverty, and the absence of a respectable Government at our back, manned by our own race, to give us the prestige of power. . . .

Men respect power; they may admire education, virtue, beauty, good manners and social embellishments, but till you show people power, they place a poor estimate upon you. As we are the most impotent and uninfluential of any member in the family of the United States, and in that ratio, less potential for good or evil, is it not our duty to put in operation such forces, experiments and expediencies as we find have been adopted by other races and oppressed people, to wring recognition from mankind in general? As I see it, we must either rebel at home or seek fortunes elsewhere. We can never acquire power sitting here quietly as menials. "Fight or run, if you will be free," is a maxim hoary with age. If the colored people of this country do not intend to fight the outrages to which they have been subjected, then, if they want to be free men, they must run for it.

There is no precedent among nations for being quiet. Be still, while you are goaded on every side, is the jargon of fools and poltroons. The language of manhood is, "Give me liberty, or give me death." A country built up in Africa to respectable proportions would be to us power in front, and respect in the rear. Besides, such a country would be an outlet for our coming young men. It would serve as a centre for missionary work, for the spread of civilization over that benighted continent. It would open a great commercial mart for the products of that, the richest of all divisions of the globe. It would be a theatre for colored officials, merchants, inventors, artisans, as well as the place where our meritorious men and women could have their names wove into prose and song, and from that centre, radiate to earth's remotest bounds.

4th. We boast of our citizenship, our civil and political rights, and legal claim to a share of the honors and glories of this country; but what does our boast amount to? Nothing but dry bombast. We are ignored by every party, and in every department of the nation. . . .

The fact is, the colored people need expect nothing in this country except what they get themselves, or through themselves. . . . [W]hile in several States South we could have had negro governors, negro senators, in short field every office with negroes, we did not do it, but came very near filling them all with white men; yet what was the sequel? These governments were held up to obloquy North, as well as South. Negro rule, negro domination, negro tyranny was the password of the country, when everybody except fools knew it was false; that white men filled nearly every position worth a cent. . . .

5th. Another reason that induces me to favor African immigration, is the well known fact that our sham Government is unable to protect its citizens. Look at how we have been slaughtered in all parts of the country; raise a howl in the North, and outrage is the order of the day. Witness a colored man last year in Indiana, killed, cut into bits, and thrown into a water-closet, upon the mere rumor that he was a party to raping some white prostitutes of the baser sort.[1] I have the newspaper reports of thirteen colored men who were lynched to death in the Northern States within the last two years, upon the

---

1. Probably the 1878 lynching of Jim Good and others in Mt. Vernon, Indiana.

mere rumor of being guilty of rape. While in the South there is no estimating the number that have been murdered, castrated, ears and nose cut off, penitentiaried for trumped up charges and other inhuman treatment. . . .

I assert and defy contradictions that in this country the negro is an outlaw. He has no rights which white men need respect, or do respect.[2] He is tried before white juries of the meaner sort, sentenced in most instances by unjust judges to the torture of hell itself, for the most trivial crimes, and ofttimes for no crime at all. His right to vote is a farce. They will kill a negro at the polls, and arrest forty others, and send half to prison, to cover up their infamy by charging insurrection upon them. In several States we are thrust into dirty, filthy cars, while we pay equal with the whites, where our wives and daughters are blackguarded and insulted by the meanest white roughs in creation. But why attempt to enumerate the infinite ills that beset us at every step? We had as well try to count the stars, or number the sands of the sea-shore.

6th. Many object to African emigration upon the ground of our poverty; they say we are too poor. Yes, but are we any poorer than the majority of whites were, who first settled in this country? Not by any means. We are told by history that thousands landed here without a cent, with wives and children, too, dependent upon them. All new countries have been settled and built up by poor people. Rich men may invest in its commerce, mines, products, etc., but the settlers are invariably poor. The same way rich men have invested in the probable wealth of other countries, they would in the prospects of African wealth. Indeed, thousands have done it already, and thousands more would be glad to do the same, if a chance was opened. . . .

This involves the question of what does the nation owe us? Let us give a minimum answer—an answer to which no reasonable person can object. The first negroes were brought to this country in 1620. They remained here in a state of slavery, until 1866, making a term of unrequited servitude of two hundred and forty-six years. At the time of their liberation they numbered four million six hundred thousand. Let us now cut off the forty-six years, and limit our servitude to two hundred years only, and to equipoise the numerical strength of our population, we will also cut off two million six hundred thousand, and suppose there were two million of us here in slavery for a term of two hundred years. And to give to each the lowest possible value, which, to

---

2. Turner alluded to the US Supreme Court's opinion, written by Chief Justice Roger B. Taney, in *Dred Scott v. Sandford* (1857), which held that African Americans "had no rights which the white man was bound to respect."

be in bounds, we will put at the annual hire of women, in anti-bellum days, each of whom averaged about one hundred dollars per year. This is to my certain knowledge. And at this minimum calculation, this country owes us forty billions of dollars—an amount that is amazing to think of, I confess. Yet, unless the Justice of God goes into eclipse, or becomes inert, this haughty nation will have to disgorge that sum in one way or another, upon the very race it has so long been holding in subjection.

I contend we have a right to demand so much of that forty billion as will start us in a national life. Better that the country pay it to us than pay it out for us in some way that will involve its reputation; for there will be no peace in this land until the manhood claim of the negro is recognized, or he leaves the bondage.

Had I the ear of the whites of this country, I would tell them that the sooner they opened the treasury of the nation and aid those who desire to leave, the sooner will peace, prosperity and harmony prevail in all sections of the land. One of three things has to come, either a wholesale intermarriage of whites and blacks, and the abolition of all caste prejudices, and a general social relation established, or they must help us to go to ourselves; for we will not remain here forever as foot-balls and spittoon-lickers. Some of our people may do it; but those of us who have grit and backbone will not. If that is not done, they had as well make up their minds to kill us out; for our children will die before they will ever endure what we have; and, as one, I hope they will. I think it my duty to so instruct my children, and shall not fail to do it.

7th. No people need expect justice in a country where all the law officers are of a different race. White people would not get it where the executive, legislative and judicial officials were all black; nor will we get it, as we too well know, where they are all white. Nor do the whites intend we shall ever have justice, otherwise they would not in nearly every state in the union resort to the vilest means to prevent us from being jurors. This is done as strenuously where the cause of action is solely with the colored as when it involves an issue between both races; showing conclusively that they do not mean right under any circumstances whatever; for it they did, why not reverse this rule sometimes, and let a colored jury determine a few white cases?

But such a thing has never been heard of in this country, otherwise a howl would have been raised all over this land, and such a revolution as it would have produced has never been heard of in this country, and who could blame them? They have a right to be tried by a jury composed in part, at least, not only of their own peers, but their own race. And, if we would do right—yes, if we were the men we ought to be—we would either have a race representative upon the juries that try us for our lives and all that is dear to man—his liberty—or set fire to every court house that dares open its doors, to put our people through the farce of a trial. There is no justice for us where we have no representative, except in the court of the God of the universe. And will you tell me to sit still and wait for better times, trust God, and pray? Such language is the wildest jargon. God would help us infinitely more by leaving such a country, than by preaching up endurance, patience and forbearance. The truth is, there is no virtue in such submission. It is just to the reverse. It is unpardonable, inexcusable, and debasing cowardice—the very thing God and nature abhors. There is not an instance in the history of men where a people ever overcame the ills that fettered them, unless they fought or emigrated to another locality. And, I repeat, that African emigration is the surest, quickest, most peaceable, most dignified, and most religious way out of our troubles.

8th. According to the newspaper reports, there is quite an exodus to the West. Thousands of our people are flying to Kansas, and to other Western States; many, too, without the means of subsistence for even a limited time. Let them go, and bid them God speed, all honor to their manhood. They are flying from injustice and wrong in every form—they are seeking the means of life, the liberties of freemen, the rights of citizens, the comforts of home, the boon of independence, the paths of elevation, the road to distinction, and, above all, a place where they can school their children and serve God in peace. Foolish and wicked men may say what they please; but they had as well tell me that the planets are tired of their orbits as to tell me our people are tired of the South. They love the South better than gold or precious gems. Born and raised in South Carolina, as I was, and living in Georgia, as I do, I know the feelings of my race; and they would never leave the South if they saw any hope for them; but they see none, and thus the exodus. Nevertheless it will only give temporary relief. The whites will crowd us out there ultimately, or subject us to the same evils, in a measure at least, that we are now trying to get rid of. And these same people, in less than fifty years, will be in search of Africa. They will, however, be far more able to go than at the present.

But let them go anywhere, rather than die in dastardly, cowardly and pusillanimous degradation. It is a very easy thing for some of our colored dignitaries, who are either in a state of fossilization or wish to pander to a class of whites, to stand away from danger and advise the colored people of the South to be still, disapprove of emigration, and hurl their bitter adjectives at the movement. But it is another thing to go in their midst, be one of them, bear, suffer, endure and die with them. They are the men the Southern negro will listen to, and they are the men he ought to listen to. I thank no man to stand on the moon and sing psalms to me, while I am contending with a cyclone or an earthquake.

9th. Lastly, I do not generally deal in imaginary fancies, or draw dark pictures for pastime. But there are terrible times ahead; another internecine war is bound to come, and that speedily. The aspect of public affairs indicates it to precision. Besides, the history of the world shows that one rebellion always succeeds another, if the first was a failure. I challenge an instance to the contrary. The threatening signs are now everywhere bicker-skirmishing before us; there is no help for it. The instability of our Government will evolve it, the innocent blood that has been shed demands it, the justice of God requires it, the pented ire of insulted heaven will urge it, and the speechless though not lifeless counterbalancing forces of nature will drive it. Yes, it will come! It will come! But in the next revolution the negro will not be a neutral spectator. He will have to suffer too, in this upheaval and rocking reign of terror, fight and die possibly, to aid in his further degradation, and for all we know to rivet upon him the gyves of his perpetual debasement. I ask if it would not be infinitely more wise to emigrate to Africa, or anywhere, if you choose, than to remain here in the face of such impending and fearful hazards?

Part Two

1880–1913

Introduction

At its 1876 General Conference, the African Methodist Episcopal (AME) Church selected Henry McNeal Turner to serve as its publication manager. Four years later, at its next General Conference, he submitted his first report in that capacity, not only highlighting his accomplishments but also discussing the hardships he faced. Among the "many discouragements," the one that "disheartened" him most was "having no credit, no money, and debts by the thousands of dollars." Nevertheless, he had succeeded "under God, in keeping the paper in weekly circulation, not missing a single issue"—a first for any manager of the department. The delegates responded by electing him the church's twelfth bishop.

As bishop, Turner had opportunities to speak all over the country, further raising his profile. At the 1885 New Orleans Exposition, he delivered "Our Brother in Black," in which he thanked the organization's planners for including African Americans. He saw this action as a rebuke of the recent US Supreme Court's ruling that the Civil Rights Acts of 1875 was unconstitutional. However, he also warned his audience that the exhibits representing Black ingenuity were not a "fair sample" of what African Americans had done and were doing. "Had we had longer time to prepare, or had the invitation not been so unexpected," he proclaimed, "we would have had an exposition here that would have been a fair representation of what the negro could do."

Two years later, Turner turned his attention to the campaign against alcohol, which was gaining momentum throughout the country. In his November 14, 1887, "Speech on Prohibition," Turner addressed more than eight thousand

people at Atlanta's Young Men's Prohibition Club. Turner grounded much
of his argument in favor of a local law banning the sale and distribution of
alcohol in religious appeals. and argued that alcohol had been a curse since
the beginning of time, asking, "Where shall the ministry stand in this campaign? If sane men, they should be on the side of prohibition."

Turner delivered the following four addresses included here at the AME
Church's New Jersey Annual Conferences between 1889 and 1891. In "Prayer
and Speech to the New Jersey Conference" (1889), Turner challenged the
church to improve its evangelizing efforts, calling for "an aggressive ministry"
and the church to "inaugurate some plan, some policy to make our work possibly more aggressive." In his "Opening Address" the following year, Turner
was more reflective: he reminded the delegates of their responsibilities and
shared some of his labors and struggles over the past year, including the death
of his wife, Eliza. Five days later, his "Ordination Sermon" highlighted the role
of prophetic ministry, speaking truth to power regardless of whether doing
so proves popular. Turner also offered his understanding of the role of pastor
as a high calling from God. Finally, in "Bishop H. M. Turner's Address," he
argued that "no lazy preacher should be kept in the itinerant ranks": for the
"lazy, sloven and don't-care minister, there is nothing him and never will be.
. . . The lazy preacher is doomed."

In the next two speeches presented, Turner addressed AME conferences in
Philadelphia and New York. In his "Opening Address" before the Philadelphia
Conference, he defended bishops against the charge that they cared only about
pastors who are "big money raisers." Turner acknowledged the importance of
money but stressed the priority of a "spiritual church" on the grounds that "the
more a church is spiritualized the more liberal the people will be. I can take a
spiritualized church and raise three times as much money from it as any man
can from a dead formal congregation. The more people are taught to respect
and reverence God, the more liberal they will be towards anything that God
enjoins." In his "Address before the New York Conference," Turner discussed
the duties expected of bishops, offered insights and wisdom to the delegates,
and challenged them to work out their issues and problems with each other.

In 1893, Turner offered the keynote address to the National Negro
Convention, a gathering held periodically beginning in 1830 at which African
Americans discussed their community's issues and concerns.[1] His "Negro
Convention Speech" related the history of the abuses that Africans and their
descendants had faced in the United States, including lynching, and offering a

wholesale critique of the country. In the light of the ongoing and unchanging oppression, Turner called for Blacks to "seek other quarters."

Two years later, Turner sounded many of the same themes in "The American Negro and His Fatherland," an address before the Congress on Africa, which focused on the continent's material and spiritual welfare and took place at Gammon Theological Seminary as part of the Cotton States and International Exposition. African Americans had no personhood future in the United States, Turner believed, as a consequence of the great chasm between Blacks and whites and an environment that led to a belief in African American inferiority and that prevented African Americans from using their intellectual acumen to build and produce in the ways they saw fit.

In his 1897 eulogy for his good friend and fellow AME bishop James C. Embry, Turner called on the church to continue Embry's legacy by producing more books and writings on the subjects of theology, hymnology, and history.

In February 1898, *Voice of Missions* published an editorial in which Turner drew on a sermon he had given on October 27, 1895. On that occasion, Turner had declared, "God is a Negro," a statement that provoked much criticism and even mockery. Standing by his words, Turner explained that "every race of people since time began who have attempted to describe their God by words, or by painting, or by carvings, or by any other form or figure have conveyed the idea that the God who made them and shaped their destinies was symbolized in themselves, and why should not the Negro believe that he resembles God as much as other people? We do not believe that there is any hope for a race of people who do not believe that they look like God."

By 1900, Turner had become frustrated with President William McKinley and the Republican Party and instead backed the Democratic presidential nominee. In his "Speech in Support of William Jennings Bryan for President," Turner declared that the Republican Party had "masqueraded as a wolf in sheep's clothing" and had "constantly lied" to African Americans. Unlike the turn-of-the-century Republicans, Lincoln "never believed in governing without the consent of the governed. He never believed in grinding down the rights and privileges of the common people. He never failed to accord honor where honor was due." Turner believed that just as Lincoln "was a friend to the colored race, so is William Jennings Bryan," who represented the "broad principles that Abraham Lincoln espoused."

In 1903, Turner delivered "Is the Pulpit Equal to the Times?" to a packed house at the People's Tabernacle in Atlanta. Using prophetic disputation,

Turner refuted points made by the Reverend Dr. H. S. Bradley, pastor of the city's influential Trinity Methodist Church, in a speech asserting that Black people had all the rights and privileges of citizens of the United States. In addition, Turner reiterated his plan for emigration.

The book closes with one of Turner's last public addresses, which I have titled "Speech at the Institutional AME Church." After being introduced before a Chicago audience in 1913, Turner asked what he should talk about. Turner displayed his gift for extemporaneous speaking, touching on subjects including the moon and the racial climate of the times.

NOTE

1. See Andre E. Johnson, "Further Silence upon Our Part Would Be an Outrage: Bishop Henry McNeal Turner and the Colored Conventions Movement," in *The Colored Conventions Movement: Black Organizing in the Nineteenth Century*, edited by P. Gabrielle Foreman, Jim Casey, and Sarah Lynn Patterson (Chapel Hill: University of North Carolina Press, 2021), 300–314.

Quadrennial Report of
Manager H. M. Turner

Delivered at the General Conference of the African Methodist
Episcopal Church of the United States, St. Louis, May 25, 1880

Source: *Journal of the 17th Session and the 16th Quadrennial Session
of the General Conference of the African Methodist Episcopal Church
in the United States, Held at St. Louis, Missouri, May 3–25, 1880* (Xenia,
OH: Torchlight, 1880)

*Turner reported on his efforts as head of the AME Church's publishing depart-
ment over the preceding four years.*

To the Members of the General Conference of the African Methodist
Episcopal Church:

In accordance with your behest, as expressed in my election at the last
session of your grave body, held in Atlanta, Ga., in the month of May 1876,
I proceeded to Philadelphia, Pa., the seat of our Publication Department,
and assumed control of the same. It may not be in apropos to state, that
after the adjournment of said General Conference, I returned to my home
in Savannah, adjusted my personal affairs with a view to leaving for my
new field of labor, and took charge of our Publishing House June 26, 1876.

Rev. W. H. Hunter, A. M., my predecessor, as per arrangement between us, remained in charge till my arrival.

A recital of my experience on taking charge of our Publishing interests would be too voluminous and multifarious to engage your attention with. Let it suffice to say, I had many discouragements, none of which disheartened me more than having no credit, no money, and debts by the thousands of dollars demanded, and all my printers taking up their hats and leaving the Department, because I could not pay them back salaries, which I found to be due them, and raise their wages immediately, which condition of things made it necessary for me to walk the streets, hunt up my printers, and beg them to come back, which they did more in sympathy for my tears, than from any desire to serve the wants of the church. Nor was I able to procure sheets of paper to print the Christian Recorder upon, till I wrote of an affidavit that I was worth at least six thousand dollars, and secured Bishop Ward and Dr. B. T. Tanner[1] to certify to it. Had I cherished the least anticipation that such a condition of things would have met me, I might have partially provided for such a contingency, though at the sacrifice of family sustenance. But without reviewing my history, labors, experiences and difficulties in the Publication Department permit me to say, that I entered upon the responsible duties of the work in one of our most trying financial times known in the history of our country, by reason of the fearful money crisis which set in about the year 1875, and continued to depress the country till 1879.[2] During that crisis eighteen publishing houses throughout the country became insolvent, and many were sold out at public auction. Besides our own Financial Secretary, with all the bishops and every minister in the church at his back, was unable to meet the salaries of our general officers at times for three and four months.

But in the face of all these odds against me, I succeeded, under God, in keeping the paper in weekly circulation, not missing a single issue during my term, being the first instance in the history of any book steward or business manager of our church. Got the new hymn book[3] in print with electrotype

---

1. Benjamin Tucker Tanner (1835–1923), editor of the *Christian Recorder*, opposed many of Turner's emigration ideas. Tanner later became a church bishop. See William Seraile, *Fire in His Heart: Benjamin Tucker Tanner and the AME Church* (Knoxville: University of Tennessee Press, 1998).

2. Probably a reference to the Panic of 1873, which caused a depression that lasted until 1879.

3. Henry McNeal Turner, ed., *The Hymn Book of the African Methodist Episcopal Church* (Philadelphia: Publication Department of the AME Church, 1877).

plates, at a cost of twelve hundred dollars for plates alone. Published a cat-echism of a hundred pages,[4] which has met with commendable sale, and gave the church such other publications as we were able, under the embarrassed circumstances surrounding us.

Many appeals were sent out through the paper at different times, to which many kind hearts favorably responded, while others did nothing but reply in taunting letters, and charge me with belittling the church by exposing my financial troubles. In this manner, however, I pushed on as best I was able, till the circulation of the Christian Recorder ran up from 1,309 copies per week, the number I found in circulation, to over 8,000 copies per week. For a few weeks I sent out 10,000 copies per week. This great increase, too, was in spite of the hard times and money pressure, and the outlook was hopeful. But in May 1877, the Financial Board, or an improvised portion of it, met in Philadelphia, and, in pursuance of the order of the General Conference, gave notes to the amount of several thousand dollars to be paid by the same. I was not apprised of the amount of these notes, nor the time of their expiration, but was glad to learn I had been relieved of the pending debts, as I had been greatly annoyed by them. This action gave me great hope, and I went to work with bright prospects, and everything ran along smoothly, till in February, 1878, while I was attending the South Carolina Conference, the sheriff, to satisfy some of these notes, levied upon the Department, and before I had any information of it, sold at auction everything in the Publication Department, and despite the efforts to keep the matter quiet, it got into the newspapers, and destroyed all the credit I had built up. For, under God, I had been successful in establishing some character for truth and veracity, and thereby had become able to command such confidence as enabled me, in case of pressing necessity, to borrow from five hundred to a thousand dollars at a time. But when the rumor went out that the Department had been sold out by the sheriff, all the reputation I had built up immediately disappeared, and I could not for a time purchase a sheet of paper without the cash. At this juncture Mr. William Steward,[5] my chief clerk, being pressed to the wall, in my absence, suspended the illustrious roll, (as I denominated the list of

---

4. Henry McNeal Turner, *Turner's Catechism* (Philadelphia: Publication Department of the AME Church, 1878).

5. William Steward (1840–1927) was Turner's chief clerk as well as a prominent author. See Eric Gardner, "William Steward's 'John Blye,'" *African American Review* 44, no. 3 (fall 2011): 337–52.

those who took papers weekly for their congregations), which gave a large number of ministers who had stood by the Department offense, and caused such a relaxation over the connection in efforts to support the Department, that a daily anticipation of suspension stared me in the face.

I struggled on, however, as best I could, till sometime in the following May, when the General Board met, and after they had given the Department the most searching examination it ever had, and approved of my report by a unanimous vote, with the consent of the Executive Board, I procured the services of Rev. Theodore Gould as Deputy Manager,[6] that I might go out and travel through the church, and gather thereby hundreds of dollars for the Department, which it was impossible to get through publishing appeals. Brother Gould accepted the position, and entered upon duty June 5th, 1878, a few days after which I left for an extensive tour, leaving Brother Gould in charge. Seeing the condition of things, no credit, and scarcely any money coming into the Department, he voluntary run his hand in his pocket, and put over a thousand dollars in the Department before I knew he even contemplated such a thing. This generous act so lubricated matters that the Department took a new start. And with such services as I could render in the field, we have gone on till the present. I have no language adequate to express my high appreciation of the services rendered by Elder Gould.

On taking charge of the Publishing House, I found that my eminent predecessor,[7] owing to the money pressure, had all the up-stairs rented out except the editor's room. I dismissed the renters, and turned the entire building into use, which I found necessary for the increasing business of the Department, except the second-story front, which some kind ladies very neatly fitted for the use of the Bishops, and is now reserved for their use, but it could be profitably used by the Department. . . .

The General Conference of 1876 ordered that ministers failing to take the *Christian Recorder*, and work for the same, should be dealt with by their Annual Conferences, as in other cases of neglect. Had this provision been carried out, the Department would have been much more successful, but in

---

6. Theodore Gould (1830–1920) succeeded Turner as manager of the publishing department in 1880.

7. William Hunter (1831–1908) was one of the first African American chaplains in the Union Army (1863–66). For more on Turner's time as publication manager, see Stephen Ward Angell, *Bishop Henry McNeal Turner and African American Religion in the South* (Knoxville: University of Tennessee Press, 1992), chapter 6.

some of our Conferences scarcely one in seven of its members have taken the paper. We hope this provision will be enforced. The same provision required the Manager to put down the name of every minister, send him the paper, and let him pay for it at his next Conference. This I did for two years, but as they failed to pay the amount of nearly $500, and some talk was had in reference to deducting the same from my wages, I resumed the cash system again. I am satisfied the credit arrangement will not work in our church.

There ought to be a steam engine and press in the Department of sufficient size to print the Christian Recorder upon, and hymn books, and Disciplines. But I have not been able to make such a purchase, owing to financial embarrassment.

We are still compelled to have our books bound outside of the Department, for the reason that we have never been able to establish a bindery. Such an office in our department, however, would be of great saving to our church.

There ought to be an addition built to the Department, which could be used as a compositors' room. Such an addition, erected with a view to that end, would be a great saving of money to the Department in gas lights alone, and a protection to health of the printers. My foreman died a few years since of diseases contracted in the present ill-arranged and uncomfortable room. Besides, it is far too small for proper use. Dr. Tanner had to give up his editorial room this last winter for the health of the printers.

We need quarters for accountant clerks, where there will be some privacy; the room they now occupy is far too small, and everyone coming into the store is almost sure to go in there; and to attempt to prevent it is sure to give insult, especially if the person is a minister. Scores of detentions, if not neglects, are due to the exposed condition of the clerks and the disposition of people to loiter around them.

The storeroom is too small and inconvenient for the wants of our department. We might make out with it, however, if the rear part now used as an office could be brought into requisition and better adapted quarters provided for the accountant clerks.

I tried to get the "Child's Recorder" in circulation, and after closely estimating the cost I discovered that if I could print 16,000 at each issue, I could cover expenses, and I called upon the church through the *Christian Recorder*, to subscribe for that number by pledges, but only 4,000 copies were called for, and I saw the project would be a loss to the department, and as I had no money to lose, or invest in a venture, I deferred the matter in the hope you would make some provision for its publication, either in money or by rigid legislation. Both may be necessary.

The time has arrived when we should start a Quarterly Review and a Ladies' Magazine. I am satisfied they could both be supported. A Quarterly Review, edited by some minister of massive brain and erudition, would find ready support and give a literature to our church now greatly needed. But for a Ladies' Magazine to succeed we will require some lady at its head. I suggest the cultured wife of some minister. Then the ministers' wives of the whole church will freely act as agents, and I believe they would sustain it far better than we do the Christian Recorder. With three or four hundred dollars to start with, and the sanction of the General Conference, such a magazine would live and prosper.

I have visited, during my term of office, several of the Conferences, viz.: Philadelphia, New Jersey, New York, New England, Pittsburgh, Ohio, Indiana, Illinois, Missouri, Kansas, Alabama, Georgia, Columbia, South Carolina, North Carolina, Virginia and Baltimore, and would have visited others had circumstances been favorable. I need scarcely to say that I presented the claims of the Department before each one of these Conferences and was not only listened to with strict attention but treated with marked respect by all. I have also preached and lectured before hundreds of congregations and tens of thousands of hearers, apparently to the gratification of those who did me the honor of listening.

How much good I did, however, is unknown to me; but I believe that through the blessing of God, if my administration has accomplished no other result, the entire church has been aroused to a concern for the department that has never marked its previous career, and the next Manager will have the advantage of more notoriety for the department, if nothing else accomplished shall be thought worthy of consideration, for the interest worked up by personal contact with the people.

A number of Ladies, through the influence of that distinguished educator and elevator of our race, Miss Fanny M. Jackson,[8] who was the President, held a bazaar in the Masonic Hall, Philadelphia, commencing November 19, 1879, for the purpose of aiding the Department, and realized by sales and donations $604.05, net. Many of these ladies, too, were members of other

---

8. Fanny M. Jackson Coppin (1837–1913) was an educator, a missionary, and the founder of the Bethel Institute in South Africa. See Fanny Jackson Coppin, *Reminiscences: School Life, and Hints on Teaching* (Philadelphia: AME Book Concern, 1913).

churches, viz.: Baptist, Presbyterian, Episcopal, as well as Methodist, and some were even Roman Catholic, showing that a universal interest is felt by all denominations and religious creeds for the perpetuity of the Christian Recorder; not so much, of course, for its denominational views, as for the fact that a large and potential paper is regarded as indispensable to our success as a people.

I am pleased to state that I have been manfully sustained by B. T. Tanner, D. D., our editor, during my term of office, and whatever differences we have had have been of opinion merely, and not of malice; for a more perfect gentleman I have never been associated with, nor do I ever covet the association of a better.

I feel it my duty to say to the General Conference, in the most emphatic terms, that it is a useless expenditure of time to pass laws to govern the Manager, and not at the same time protect him from the many disadvantages taken of him; for there will be no success. I care not who may go into office, till the church realizes that this Department is a mighty factor of our connection, and all necessary contingencies are provided for. . . .

It might be thought impertinent in me to recommend my successor, as the judgment of so grave a body as yours is far more competent to determine the relative merits of its members than mine. But as I desire to be released from the Department, because of the perpetual annoyance and vexation of the position, and yet, knowing that someone acquainted with the duties ought to remain in the office, I most respectfully beg to recommend Rev. Theodore Gould. He has been with me nearly two years and understands the office work thoroughly; and is prompt in business, and I am sure would make you a good Manager.

Thank you for the honor of calling me to the head of the Publication Department, also for the reception given to the new hymn book which I had the honor of compiling, and the recognition given to the Turner Catechism, and other labors I have tried to render the church.

Our Brother in Black

Delivered at the World Cotton Centennial, New Orleans,
February 27, 1885

SOURCE: *Washington National Republican*, February 28, 1885

*Between December 1884 and June 1885, New Orleans hosted the World Cotton
Centennial, a fair commemorating the one hundredth anniversary of the first
recorded shipment of cotton from the United States to England. The exposition's director general, Edward A. Burke (1839–1928), a former Confederate
soldier who had been involved in an attempted coup against New Orleans's
integrated city government in 1874, invited African Americans to participate,
and Turner eagerly accepted. He took the opportunity not only to laud Burke
for his efforts at inclusion but also to cast those efforts as a rebuke to the US
Supreme Court's October 1883 ruling that parts of the Civil Rights Act of 1875
were unconstitutional.*[1]

I am quite unprepared to speak to you on this occasion, but as I stand here
to-day, surrounded by the result of 6,000 years of human effort and experience, by every variety of manufacture, by sculptures and paintings, and

---

1. For more on Turner and the Supreme Court, see Andre E. Johnson, *No Future in This
Country: The Prophetic Pessimism of Bishop Henry McNeal Turner* (Jackson: University Press
of Mississippi, 2020), chapter 1.

every department of science; as I stand here and recognize the fact that the colored race has been invited for the first time to contribute its little share, no matter how meager it might be, to the great Exposition, I would be an ingrate before God and man were I not to feel some gratification, to feel like uttering some words of pleasure.

When the colored people were first invited to take part in the exposition I could scarcely believe that I understood aright, knowing how we had been cold-shouldered in the past and knowing how the supreme court had turned us over to the roughs on the public highways by virtue of the decision in the civil rights case. I could not believe that in Louisiana, in New Orleans, in the Crescent City, there was a man known as Director Gen. Burke, and that there were other men associated with him on the board of management, who would rebuke this unjust decision of the supreme court and would advocate the recognition of our manhood and of our citizenship in the manner in which they have. The name of Director Gen. Burke will be enshrined in the gratitude of the negro for all time to come. I could draw a picture of the status of the colored people of this country. I know it as well as any man that breathes the breath of life; I know that we have been made hewers of wood and drawers of water; that we have been precluded from all positions of honor and merit; that we have been permitted to do nothing but wait at table and perform other menial services, and to plow and hoe in the fields. I do not depreciate the occupation of a farmer or of those who labor under him; I think the cultivation of the fruits of the earth is the grandest and noblest of all occupations. But the theory has been heretofore held up before the world that the negro lacked the ability that would entitle him and qualify him to fill the rank of a skilled laborer in the scale of society.

But the people of the south, the very people whom the supreme court had in view when they issued that heaven-daring decision, are now saying to the colored man in this Exposition: "Come, let us see what you have done during these twenty years; come and join hands with us." I thank God that the very heart of the south has rebuked that decision of the supreme court. I am proud of that exhibition of industry and of art that I saw upstairs in the government building.

But do not let it be taken as a fair sample of what the negro has done, and of what he is doing. Remember that, as I presume, we were not thought of in the first programme, and that, when the invitation came it was so unexpected, so marvelous, so Utopian that we could scarcely believe it was true. Had we had longer time to prepare, or had the invitation not been so unexpected, we would have had an exposition here that would have been a fair representation of what the negro could do.

I have preached and I have written that there is no future in this country for the colored man; but I must say that if the white people of this country, instead of maligning and misrepresenting us from day to day as they have hitherto very generally done, would fling open the doors of their institutions, would admit us into the great arena of human effort and activity and genius instead of judging us before they examine us—why, I don't know after all but what I might somewhat modify my radical ideas.

The American nation understands how to let the negro die in defense of her government, but it does not understand how to preserve to the negro his rights of citizenship in traveling on the common highway. But Director General Burke and the gentlemen connected with this Exposition have rebuked the supreme court for its decision, have stretched out their hands to us, and have said: "Come and join us; we will treat you right." And they have kept their word. I have not been snubbed since coming here. I cannot believe that I am in New Orleans. I am inclined to think it must be all a dream. All honor, I say, to Director General Burke. All honor to the managers of this Exposition. All honor to New Orleans.

All honor to the south for the consideration they have shown to the colored race, for their answer to the abominable proclamation of the supreme court.

A Speech on Prohibition

Delivered at the Warehouse (Prohibition Headquarters), Atlanta,
November 14, 1887

SOURCE: *Atlanta Constitution*, November 15, 1887

*Frustrated with the Republican Party, Turner briefly turned his attention to
Prohibition, giving this speech before an antiliquor gathering held in advance
of an Atlanta vote on whether to ban alcohol.*

I beg no pardon for appearing here tonight, humble minister though I
be. I know that the advocates of liquor and all its evil consequences have
become exceedingly fastidious, and much concerned about the dignity of
the ministry. . . .

I am not addressing the crowd I would like. It would have pleased me to
have seen a large number of the advocates of liquor present. They are disap-
pearing like ice before the sun. . . .

I am here to reason, and not abuse. I will not villify the liquor men as they
have traduced the ministry. I pity them, and sympathize with them. But should
there be barrels of alcohol here, I will hurl thunderbolts in your face. . . .

Where shall the ministry stand in this campaign? If sane men, they should
be on the side of prohibition. If they are idiots or madmen I will excuse
them, and God will excuse them. What does this campaign mean? What is its

object? It is for the overthrow of alcohol, call it by what name you will, and sell it where you may, in filthy doggeries or in glided saloons. It is the same old alcohol. If alcohol is right we should stand by it; if wrong, we should reject it.

What has been the history of alcohol since its birth? It has cursed man from the crown of his head to the sole of his feet; it has cursed his hair, his eyes, his lips, his tongue, his brain, his heart, his lungs, his flesh, his tissues and his intellect; it alienates him from his God, shortens his life and damns his soul.

That alcohol has a place in commerce and in mechanical arts, I will not dispute. Possibly under some remote circumstances it may be of some little assistance in the medical world, but I doubt it so much that I don't believe it.

Alcohol may be used in a thermometer when you go to the north pole. It has so much of hell in it it does not care to freeze.

God never inspired man to discover an art that mankind didn't need for 5,000 years, for before its introduction men lived to be 900 years of age, and generals, poets and giants lived and flourished without it. We are told to use it in winter to keep us warm and in summer to keep us cool. God and nature is opposed to its use.

How did it get such a hold upon man? How many millions of men it has destroyed! How many tears it has wrung from woman, that cherub wrapped in flesh and handed down to men! It has wrung tears enough from mothers, wives, daughters and sisters to float the British navy, and if collected together in one place and descending on Atlanta would drown every living thing and sweep away every building.

God never made a blind man, a deaf man, or caused a child to die from a little sickness. This is always the result of a violated law by the parents.

Alcohol not only curses the parent, but goes on to drag his posterity down to ruin. We blame God for it, when it is the result of the infamous old barroom.

The crowd here tonight tells us that victory is perching on our banners in advance.

Man is naturally a centenuarian.

Moses wrote that song about man's life being three score years and ten when the Israelites were dying from malaria and sojourning in the desert. All animals live five times the number of years it takes to reach maturity. A man is more than an animal, and has a right to live five times twenty years.

We will arrest the monster before we have done and preach the funeral.

The antis are falling in love with the Bible. They have studied it more in the past two years than they have done since 1805. Every anti carries a Bible in his pocket, and oh, how they can quote Scripture.

The first instance we read in the Bible of the use of wine is when Noah got drunk and hurled his curses. The white people said that the curses fell upon Ham and turned all the negroes black. If that is a fact the negroes ought to hate liquor until the day of their death. Lot got drunk and was guilty of the gravest crime known to the law. Nadab and Abihu got drunk and were struck dead. The blights, disgraces and judgment of God fell upon these men....

I have brought a Bible along. Hear what God says to Aaron, the father of Nadab and Abihu, and their posterity forever:

"Do not drink wine nor strong drink nor thy sons with thee lest thou die."[1]

Some say that this was only intended for the priests. God has only one law, and that governs alike both priest and people.

Hear what is said in the Book of Proverbs:

"Who hath woe? Who hath sorrow? They that tarry long at the wine; they that seek mixed wine."[2]

In the 5th chapter of Isaiah, we have the following:

"Woe to them that rise early in the morning and go to seek strong drink, till wine inflame them."[3]

The Hebrew Bible gives it "running after strong drink."

Habakkuk declares, "Woe unto him that giveth his neighbor drink."[4]

The Hebrew bible renders it "that maketh his neighbor drink."

One of the distinguishing characteristics of John the Baptist was that he should "neither drink wine nor strong drink."[5] Eighteen hundred years ago fermented wine met the divine disapproval.

When the antis tell you that whisky has been here always, since the world was made, he either tells a blatant falsehood or advertises his own ignorance. How old is alcohol? The sages, patriarchs and wise men of the ages knew nothing of it. Greece and Rome never heard of it. Humanity lived 5,210 without it. It was 1,246 years after the birth of Christ before it was discovered. A

---

1. Leviticus 10:9.
2. Proverbs 23:29–30.
3. Isaiah 5:11.
4. Habakkuk 2:15.
5. Luke 1:15.

dram shop was unknown until 1561. The use of whisky is only about three hundred years old.

It is claimed that alcohol is good medicinally. [It is good for snake bites:] Yes, my friend, it takes one deadly poison to neutralize another one. Let them neutralize each other and not destroy the man. The discoverer of alcohol should never have termed it water of life. He should have named it water of death.

You are told that you must vote for whisky in order to vote your liberty. Oh, liberty, hast thou come down and got into a whisky barrel? Should you defeat prohibition, can you establish a barroom at every corner. You won't have the liberty to do so, without obtaining a license to do so, from, I don't know how many sources. There is no liberty. Every man, woman and child are under the law.

The sun, moon and ocean are under law. The comets, God's inspector generals, are under law. It will be a high time if you are turned loose.

Can you point me to a missionary in China or Africa sustained by a barroom, or a schoolhouse erected by them?

You that vote for alcohol, vote for murder, poverty, curses and wife beating. Will you manufacture drunken sons-in-laws for your daughters?

I'm not a prohibitionist because I am a preacher, but because alcohol will shorten my life, burn my brain and paralyze my liver.

The women are unanimously on the side of prohibition. I did hear a few unfortunate wrecks say on the street, "I'm wet." But they are so few that they are not in our way.

Did you ever see so many rag-tags as has cropped out lately? I have not seen them for two years. Where did they come from? They certainly did not come from Heaven. After the last contest I met them in Birmingham, Chattanooga and other places. They were telling horrid tales about Atlanta's loss of wealth and grass growing in her streets. The wonder is that this result was not attained in consequence of the howl raised by these men.

I will say to the colored men, that their reputation is at stake.

The antis say that they will buy us up. Are we for sale? I hope not. I'm told that certain men are employed by the antis to pay voters twenty cents! They are a little leaner than they were before. Are we to be bought for twenty cents?

But the objection is urged that the prohibitionists did not put on negro policemen. There are negro policemen in Memphis, Nashville, Chattanooga, Charleston, Richmond and Wilmington.

When alcohol is put in one end of the scale, and the little old dry police-man's place (I mean no reflection on the police) put in the other, I would never vote for alcohol. Everybody could not get on the force, and those that didn't get on wouldn't like those that did. Then, we know one another so well that it is better that colored policemen were not on the force. They would find out more than white men ever dreamed of. There is no more comparison between liquor traffic and a policeman's place than there is between hell and heaven. When you vote against whisky do you vote for the white people?

It is the foolishness of folly to say otherwise.

I compliment the white folks, in that they did not give us whisky when they owned, us and kept us sober. We always had to get a pass, and that was right. We could work all day and dance all night. We are voting for ourselves, our wives, our children, our pockets and for heaven and against hell. When I advocated the right of my race to cast the ballot, why Turner was a big man, but when I tell them how to cast that vote, I'm meddling with politics. I'm talking to the man on the wrong side.

Some say that they can't understand it. In time of slavery, ignorance was our only defense. We beat the white man many times by being ignorant. The reason is you want to do wrong and haven't the courage to look a man in the face and say yes, I will.

A man who buys a negro for a fool will lose his money, unless he's a victim of alcohol—then he'll do anything.

I saw a procession of colored antis in Tennessee; three hundred of them, fringed in rags, behind a banner bearing this inscription: "The constitution of the fathers is good enough for us."

A speaker at the artesian well indulged in the following language, I am told: "I don't care if God and his whole family gets drunk." It is said a thousand black and white men observed it. Can you follow such a crowd?

Prohibition does prohibit with all honest, law-abiding men. Men with a sense of honor, shows that the antis are dodging and justly belong to that class whose sphere is the penitentiary.

The antis ridicule woman. Without her the world would be a desert. She inspires and prompts man to every noble deed. She is the mother of human-ity; nay more, the mother of Jesus Christ, the Redeemer of the world. She was made as a helpmeet, fit for him, to be eyes, hands and soul to him. A single man is only half a man, and an old bachelor is a monstrosity.

The women are wearing the blue. The sky, the universe, the ocean, are blue. I thank God the prohibitionists selected blue.

Red represents war, carnage and death, and you'll get it, too, if whisky is voted back. The tatterdemalions now crying out for whisky will be in their graves or in the penitentiary in less than a year.

I believe that God in bringing the black man here had a grand purpose in view. By bringing us in contact with the Caucasian race (Japhet now rules), religion and the Bible will make of us a great race, and build up a civilization that God Almighty will approve. The sober, thoughtful white men are willing to aid us in getting on the platform of sobriety. Shall we turn our backs on it? We have got to bring Africa to God, and the destruction of the whisky traffic is the first step in the grand work we are to accomplish.

Jefferson Davis[6] is your hero. I don't blame you for honoring him. He was the negative of a positive force that resulted in your emancipation. Abraham Lincoln is the negro's hero. Neither race objects to the other worshipping their own hero.

It is claimed that Lincoln was an anti. He used to sell liquor, and sold it to Stephen A. Douglas.[7] But in 1846 or 1847 he joined the temperance army and remained in it to his death. With his own hand during the war he wrote passes for temperance speakers to go into the camps. What did he say to a colored delegation? "Tell your people that they are now free, and if they let liquor alone and take care of their earnings there is a future for them." The logic of this is that is if they did not, they had no future.

Will you heed, my colored friends, heed the advice of Abraham Lincoln or Jefferson Davis?

---

6. Jefferson Davis (1808–89) served as president of the Confederate States of America (1861–65).

7. Stephen A. Douglas (1813–61) was a member of the US House of Representatives (1843–47) and the US Senate (1847–61). He ran unsuccessfully for president in 1860, losing to Abraham Lincoln.

Prayer and Speech to the
New Jersey Conference

Delivered at the New Jersey Annual Conference of the African
Methodist Episcopal Church, Mt. Holly, May 1, 1889

SOURCE: *Journal of the Seventeenth Session (After Organization) of the
New Jersey Annual Conference of the A.M.E. Church, Held at Mt. Holly,
N.J., from May 1st to May 7th, 1889* (Philadelphia: Power, 1889)

In this keynote address, Turner focused on the church's evangelizing efforts.

Prayer:

Oh, thou who art God, who rulest the heavens and inhabitest the earth, we
come on bended knees with faces, hearts and hands turned toward heaven to
engage the attention of the Lord, our Maker. We render to Thee the thanks of
our hearts for the blessings that have followed through our lines down to this
moment. After a year's labor and separation—after a year's experience and
toil—after a year's battle and turmoil in many instances, we have met together
in another conference session. Last year we met face to face with some who
were present before, but are absent now; with whom we will meet no more.
But we bless Thy holy name that so many of us have been spared; that we
have passed through dangers visible and invisible since Thou hast put us to
the test. O Lord, our God, we come humbly to a throne of grace. Thou hast

rendered Thy mercy towards us, but all we can do is to order the course of our lives and the gratitude of our hearts to Thee. Whatever we have done amiss forgive and pardon us for the Redeemer's sake. Baptize us in these sessions by Thy Holy Spirit that our meeting maybe profitable; that its influence and power and application shall tend to [t]he salvation of souls now and in days to come. Oh, Lord God, bless each minister present and those who have not yet arrived; may we spend the time here to the glory of Thy name and in the interest of the Church. Help us to control our temper, to restrain our passions, bridle our tongues. Throw around about us Thy mantle of love that we may be received up into the glory of God. Let us not be vindictive, nor revengeful, nor spiteful; may we remember who we are and our high calling, that God may be glorified. We pray Thee to bless our Church everywhere and all of them who preach the Word of God and offer salvation through Jesus Christ. Bless these ministers, we beseech Thee, here and elsewhere. Bless us while we are here and when we shall go away from this place may we go away determined to work for God. May God stand for us in our responsibility. Give us concerted brains, Christianized hearts and sanctified lives. May our lives be in harmony with the gospel. May every notion and power that impels us be in the right direction; may we be truly messengers of the Cross. We pray, therefore, for all conditions of men of every land and every clime. We pray Thee especially for the heathen world, and especially to raise up men who shall feel an interest in affairs and in sending the Gospel to that benighted land. We pray for such as are in confinement[,] for such as are suffering the penalties for offences committed against the law, and if they cannot satisfy the demands of the law of the land, may they have pardon through Jesus Christ, be fitted to rise on high, and when done with the world take charge of us, guide and direct us and ultimately save us through Christ. Amen.

Address:

BRETHREN.—In the providence of God, I trust, I am with you in another relation from what I held when I visited you last year at Millville, I came then as a visitor in the discharge of some business rather of a personal nature between myself and Bishop Campbell.[1] It was the least of my expectations that I would be so early sent to you, charged with responsibilities. It is true that the Bishops of our church are responsible everywhere, in any part of the world, much more in any portion of the church; and particularly now

---

1. Jabez Pitt Campbell (1815–91) was a bishop of the AME Church (1864–91).

since the little bickerings have been settled in regard to the British Methodist Episcopal Church;[2] that was the only bar, the only chasm that separated us from the entire globe. The last General Conference, however put the quietus to that, and affirmed what they had legislated and ultimately effected before. Now there is no limitation, nor bar that would seem to limit the territory of any bishop in the church. In fact it does not. If you can settle that, you have our abnormal legislation upon the matter. I have visited several of your charges during the year, and others would have been visited had it been possible. Many invitations have been extended with which I could not comply. Possibly I would have done more good had I gone to some of the other places. Water cannot rise above its level, and a man cannot rise above his judgment. He must simply decide for himself at a certain point, matters that are brought for his consideration. Now I am in your midst, a feeble instrument in every respect. No man feels the necessity for higher religion and education more than I do. I do not come to you, Brethren with any idea that I can succeed without your assistance and co-operation. I am open to advice and counsel. I may not always be guided by your advice, for when I conscientiously differ from you, I shall follow my own convictions. It may be a mistake. Making a man a bishop does not put any more brains in his head than he had before. I have been a licentiate, deacon and elder, and now I am a Bishop. When I was a deacon I was somewhat of a scholar and was somewhat versed in the classics; when I became an elder I did not know more than I had learned; and now since I have got to be a Bishop I know less, for there are so many things to absorb my mind that I do not have time to study.

I wish to say to the Conference, I am in your midst. If God permits me to remain in the church and to live, and nothing happens for four years, I

---

2. The AME Church formed a conference in Canada in 1840. A decade later, after the United States passed the 1850 Fugitive Slave Act, many Canadian preachers had concerns about traveling south of the border. In 1856, the AME Church created the British Methodist Episcopal Church (BMEC), with Willis Nazery as its first bishop. After Nazery's death in 1875, the church chose Richard Randolph Disney (1830–91), and the AME Church ordained him a bishop of the BMEC. In 1880, Disney called for a reunion with the AME Church. While the motion was ratified at the 1881 BMEC convention, much of the opposition came from members in Ontario, which led those churches to reestablish the BMEC. In 1886, the Ontario churches broke away from the AME Church and renounced Disney as bishop. Disney continued to serve other AME churches in Canada until 1888, when the church moved him to the Arkansas and Mississippi district. He subsequently contracted malaria there and died. See Dennis C. Dickerson, *The African Methodist Episcopal Church: A History* (New York: Cambridge University Press, 2020).

shall try to serve you faithfully. But should I, in the providence of God, be called away as was your former Bishop—Bishop Cain—that would close our relations sooner. I am sure to do the best I can for the church of God. I am intensely concerned about our Church everywhere. I think I have been instrumental in doing some good in the past, and I shall render you the best services I possibly can in the future. With the large districts, covering extensive territory, it is impossible for a Bishop to reach every charge. I do, however, see from the little experience that I have had, that some things should be done, some measures should be inaugurated to make our ministerial labors more aggressive on the one hand and more successful on the other. I say what I am going to say, kindly and tenderly, and if there are any Baptists in the Church, I trust they will take no offence at it. My mother was a Baptist, and I was converted in the Baptist Church. I am a Methodist now, and I think something on this order will ultimately capture the world. I have nothing against the Baptists. I bid them God speed. There are plenty of sinners for them to get. I do not care what church people may attend, if the ministers preach repentance toward God and faith in the Lord Jesus Christ. But I see no reason why we should sit down here supinely and quietly allow the Baptists to eat us up. My attention has been called again and again to places where they are getting the better of us with all our possibilities, and you know we love to work. I have no objection to a man thinking well of himself; I have no objection to our Church thinking well of itself. This African Methodist Church is a grand organization. I am proud of it; but our Baptist brethren are outrunning us in this State and in parts of Delaware. We may laugh at their ignorance, their groans and moaning and their manner of worship, but I know from traveling over the district and from observation, that in many places they are outrunning us. There is no reason why we should not equal them in every particular. I am not advocating that kind of church rivalry that means the downfall of any society, that means to advance by pulling another down. I fear our race is somewhat cursed with that spirit. Some of them desire to rise upon dead men's bones. I thank God I will not have that sin to answer for at the judgment. When I speak of this denomination as our preference I do not mean to utter a sentence nor say a word in any manner to the detriment of any other church; but I do say that there is no need in the world in quietly sitting by and allowing another denomination, in many places, to eat us up, as I have seen done right here in New Jersey and down in Delaware.

Brethren, we want an aggressive ministry, and the best thing we can do is to inaugurate some plan, some policy to make our work possibly more aggressive. The places that I have visited, and the ministers with whom I have talked, almost without an exception have been full of ideas, full of suggestions, full of plans with reference to the situation. Of course we differ as men naturally will, but I do hope and trust that we will during this session do something, legislate somehow, maneuver in some way for the best interest of the church. Every minister in charge is a general, colonel or captain. He is at the head of an army. Every pastor has been acting as a general during the year. It is your business as commander of your respective armies to study, plan, maneuver and advise in every way to beat the devil and bring men to God.

Now as we are here in a Conference session let us be dignified, gentlemanly and courteous in our bearing. I believe you will be so, and I only remind you of the necessity of it in passing. It does no harm to repeat good advice. I do not know after all but in many instances it inspires our loyalty and generates within us a kind of spirit of devotion and allegiance that will sometimes die out if not encouraged. There will be discussions. We are here to talk, to exchange views and to dispute in our differences. Variety is the order of nature. No two grains of sand are alike. No two leaves are alike. Out of the millions of stars that exist no two are alike. While we differ, let us remember that we all belong to the same army. I remember while in North Carolina, just before the fight at Bentonville,[3] there was a big row kicked up in the regiment. A number of men were fighting with each other, and the officers had drawn their swords and rushed among the men to separate them, when all at once the long roll was sounded. They looked up and saw the rebels coming down upon them and they ceased immediately to contend with one another and turned their attention to the common enemy. That is the way we must do. Let us remember that we are Methodist ministers; that we are African Methodist ministers. Let all your discussions be gentle and courteous. I entreat you to use no harsh terms if avoidable. Quote as much Scripture as possible and ransack the records of the world to establish a point. Bring all the energy you can into the discussions and at the same time believe that the man with whom you are arguing is a gentleman and a Christian. I thank God for your attention and patience, and I pray the blessings of God upon each and all of you and those committed to your care.

---

3. The Battle of Bentonville, March 19–21, 1865, in Johnston County, North Carolina, was a decisive Union victory in the waning weeks of the Civil War.

Opening Address

Delivered at the New Jersey Annual Conference of the African Methodist Episcopal Church, Mt. Zion Church, New Brunswick, April 30, 1890

SOURCE: *Southern Christian Recorder*, May 22, 1890

In this more reflective address, Turner reminded conference attendees of their responsibilities and shared his struggles over the past year, including the death of his wife, Eliza.

Brethren of the New Jersey Annual Conference:— After another year of separation, labors, experience and afflictions, fears within and fightings without, we assemble this side of the grave in another annual conference. We are here to make a report, a partial report of our labors for one year; getting ready to make a life time report in the presence of the Church of all the earth. Our experiences have naturally been varied. We have had the heat of summer and the cold of winter. Some have endured privations and others have had many smiles lavished upon you. Opponents have confronted us at times when our motives were good—when we thought our endeavors were for the best. Their position may have been correct and ours may have been incorrect, and yet as water cannot rise above its level, we can see plainly that it will redound to the glory of God and to the good of the church—that it will result in blessing our fellow men. We are often inclined to think that those who differ with us are possibly trying to throw stumbling blocks in our way. In too many instances this is the case; and in too many instances we are too uncharitable. We should take the most charitable view of everything and everybody. Let us remember that it is only through the mercies of God that most of us are here today.

I hope that while the conference is in session that each and every one of us will demean ourselves in accordance with the dignity of the occasion and our high calling. We are representatives of the Lord Jesus Christ—we are the mouth pieces of him who hung upon the cross, and who intercedes for us on high. Our station is exalted. We attach wonderful importance to ministers plenipotentiary sent out of the United States to represent this country. It is an honorable distinction, but it is earthly. It is nothing more than business. It is the discharge of certain temporal duties. It is filling no higher sphere than any other man following the ordinary pursuits of life; but we go out as representatives of the Lord of Hosts to proclaim his word—to invite people to come and serve him, and to get ready to worship him in heaven. I trust that every one of us has done this to the best of our ability. My labors have been abundant. My experiences since I met with you have been fearful. I have passed through an ordeal of which I never before had any proper conception. That little angel that was with me at the last session of the conference, my wife, whom you all saw is no more in the land of the living. She took her departure since our last session, and has gone to the climes of uncloudless bliss. If I could believe that faithful christian wife did not enter through the pearly gates, I would sit down in sackcloth and ashes and in dispair.

I have visited some of you and several of you I have not visited during the past year. I have been busy day and night. I can say truthfully, I have eaten no idle bread. I have visited every point I could, and I have answered hundreds of letters pertaining to the general interests of the church. True I was out of my district, working for the best part of three months, helping Bishop Disney, whose physical condition needed assistance. Knowing his affliction and in keeping with the action of the Bishops' council, I went to his relief, and in doing so I was laboring in the vineyard of the Lord and Master as best I could. Though I have not had the opportunity of visiting you all, I hope I shall be able to do so this year, or the greater portion of you.

I am warned to be careful and prudent. For the first time in my life, I have felt my health and strength giving away. I have staggered at nothing. God gave me an iron constitution, . . . and I have utilized it for many long years in the pulpit, on the platform as a lecturer, as a chaplain in the army, as a pioneer of our work in the southwest portion of the country. I did not stagger nor falter nor fear anything, but I put my trust in the great head of the church and went everywhere. I am now getting along in years, though I am not as old as Methuselah; but I have felt for the first time that I am breaking down.

The doctors have told me that I need four months of rest. I have been advised to take it. I am not much concerned whether I live or die. Since my wife died, I prayed for about five months to die, but God would not answer my prayers. Though I have not visited all of you, I judge all of the presiding elders have been to the respective charges under their administration. I trust they were profitable visitations. Every one of you know the schedule and duties of the presiding eldership. I am very glad to say in the main that while there has been some grumbling, I have heard a thousand blessings on my district following the appointment of presiding elders. It is rather new in this part of the district. You have had pastors with the oversight of districts; but I mean to say that you have never had before full fledged presiding elders. The office is necessary to the spirit of Methodism. If white people with all their culture and progress need it north and south, and have utilized since the foundation of Methodism in this country, how much more necessary is it for African Methodists? The venerated Asbury,[1] who was a Bishop in the Methodist Episcopal Church, was a presiding elder fifteen years before he was a deacon; and yet if they have found it necessary to the perpetuation of their church, it is evident that we are in greater need of power. The very men who grumble against the system of presiding eldership are those who need it most. I sometimes question them as to their duties and responsibilities; and if they answer the first question they generally fail on the second as to the law, their duties and with reference to church government. I could tell you a little story that would be amusing, but I shall not take the time to do so. Sometimes indiscreet men render a good system unpopular, and we often fail to discriminate between man and the system he represents. We often in our prejudice condemn the cause, when really our opposition is only against the man who is trying to advance it. Do not oppose a principle because you dislike the man who represents it. Do not fall out with all women because

---

1. Francis Asbury (1745–1816) was one of the first two bishops of the Methodist Episcopal Church in the United States.

your wife proves to be unworthy, nor would it be generous on the part of the ladies to condemn all men because some rough man beats his wife. Judge a system upon its merits, and of an individual by his worth. I am prepared to say had the presiding eldership been established in the early history of our church, and had the presiding elders been intelligent, fatherly and dutiful, administering their office in the true spirit of Methodism, we would have three churches where we now have one. There are some churches that have a greater missionary spirit than others, and they need a controlling influence to direct their operations; and under the administration of a judicious presiding elder they are bound to succeed. I entreat you to be earnest in the work, in building up missions, circuits and stations in the best interest of the people and for the advancement of the Redeemer's kingdom. Now brethren, I have detained you a little longer than I intended. Let us enter upon the duties of the conference in the proper spirit. Let each one labor to perform well his part, so that when we depart from this city, we will, by our influence, leave the people better spiritually.

Ordination Sermon

Delivered at the New Jersey Annual Conference of the African Methodist Episcopal Church, Association Hall, New Brunswick, May 4, 1890

SOURCE: *Southern Christian Recorder*, May 29, 1890

In this sermon, Turner preached from Jeremiah 3:15: "And I will give you pastors according to my heart, which shall feed you with knowledge and understanding."

... Jeremiah came on the stage just at the time when God was withdrawing his word from his chosen people. If my recollection serves me alright, it was about the time that Josiah slew Pharoah—nechoch. Jehoiakim was anointed king; but he followed in the footsteps of his father, and wandered away from God. We learn that Jeremiah went before him and shook his finger in his face and told him of the coming judgments. God told him to stand upon the porch of the temple as the people came, and proclaim his word and warn them of the coming judgments—that the heathen king would capture the people, capture Solomon's temple, and that the government would be overthrown; that the sacred treasures that have been preserved, the ark of the covenant, and all the memorable emblems that they brought out of Egypt will all be carried off never to be returned. This period of the downfall of the peculiar people was just about the birth of the Roman empire, which event God intended to utilize in the coming day. Because of his righteousness

Jeremiah was hated. Jehoiakim did not do very much to him because he was afraid. But Zedekiah did put him in prison. The people claimed that he was a very wicked man because he stated the truth. There were many prophets in his day; but nobody supported him but Urigah. All of the others were popular dudes and spoke to please the people. God have mercy on such preachers. Instead of standing up for the right and against the wrong, this kind of ministers are seeking popularity at the expense of their own souls and the souls of the people. They cannot see farther than their pockets—how far their living may be effected, and which way the smiles of the people are turned. I trust young men, who are to be ordained to-day, that you will hear what I am saying to you. The country was full of prophets in the days of Jeremiah; and because his prophecies did not please the people, Zedekiah cast him into prison as many as three times. The last time he was in prison he was consigned to the deep and damp dungeon of Malachiah with the view to his destruction; and where he came near being suffocated. He put his trust in God and resolved to be true to his convictions. He recanted nothing, and Zedekiah, doubtless being moved upon by a higher power, sent thirty men to rescue Jeremiah from his tomb. When the prophet came into the presence of Zedekiah he asked Jeremiah, what message have you from your God? Then Jeremiah said unto Zedekiah, "If I declare it unto thee, wilt thou not surely put me to death? The prophet was oppressed and dispirited, but he was determined to tell the truth or nothing. He said in effect, let me hold my peace; but if I must speak, promise me my life. The king secretly swore unto Jeremiah that we would not put him to death, and neither would he deliver him into the hands of those who desired his life. Jeremiah gave Zedekiah, king of Judah, to understand that he should be carried into Babylon, if he did not go forth to the king of Babylon's princes, and that his country should be destroyed and overrun with the enemies. The prophets told such as would hear him and listen that their only hope was to go, for God is going to put you to an ordeal for resistance to his laws. All of the signs are against you, said the prophet, and the frown of God is upon you.

This brings me without further narrative to address you upon the words I have selected this morning. When Jeremiah was speaking or writing either in prison or elsewhere, he called on backsliding Israel to repent. O ye backsliders, ye wanderers from God, after so much had been done for you, return, and come to our Saviour: and then he told them what the Lord had promised, if they would consecrate their hearts, he would give them pastors after his

own heart. Do you know what the word pastor signifies? It does not simply mean a teacher or a preacher; but in the sense that Jeremiah used it, it
means a king, a sovereign and whatever position of power should be given
to man. The religion of the Israelites, of the Hebrews was not founded upon
theory. I despise the religion of this country as it is practiced, whatever I may
think of its profession. To be a successful and popular christian minister is
to be very dudish, and to over look the faults of the people. He can go up
to heaven and down to hell in his sermons, but do not touch these liquor
stalls; do not touch the iniquity of the government in not protecting them;
do not touch the injustice of the Nation's supreme court; do not touch the
desecration of the Sabbath day because certain municipalities have granted
certain privileges for dissipation in the sunlight of heaven: do not touch the
popular sins of the land, nor anything that is likely to come home to the
people. Do not dabble with politics. Great heaven! what is it? I stand here to
day to tell you, young men that every thing in heaven, earth or hell is within
your line of duty for consideration and discussion. I tell you that you are to
study men—study what God would have you say—analyze every principle,
every law and everything pertaining to the welfare of the people. Find out
whether it is right or wrong. Take it and compare it with God's world, and
weigh it in the scales of divine justice, and if it cannot stand the test, let the
missels of destruction and death be hurled against it. But God says, I will give
you laborers—I will give you pastors—I will give you an instruction after my
own heart. O! let us look at that a little while. Much has been said about the
call to the ministry. I used to read Dr. Talmage's[1] sermons until he said that
the call to the ministry was no more than a call to be a doctor, a lawyer, a
farmer or any other secular pursuit. When I read that I stopped reading Dr.
Talmage's sermons, and do not expect to read another one. Any man who
has no more conception of a ministerial calling than Dr. Talmage is not a
pastor after God's heart, and is unable to feed the people with knowledge and
understanding. I care not what his intellectual brilliancy may be, he cannot
realize heaven's idea of a pastor while he entertains such views. There must
be a deep seated trust in God and a comprehension of his will to be a pastor
after God's own heart. I shall not occupy time this morning to discuss this
idea elaborately; but I tell you that God Almighty lays his hand upon such

---

1. Thomas De Witt Talmage (1832–1902) was a popular US preacher in the middle and
late nineteenth century.

men as he proposes to help him before his people. . . . Look at everything broadly, charitably and pitiously; not all the time presuming unfavorably and hunting for some defects and some shortcomings; thinking that some one is trying to trick you, or endeavoring to beat you. God Almighty have mercy upon you, and give us to day a trust in the arm of that power that rules the universe. I could easily presume evil of others and find fault with the machinery of this life and other things upon this earth where we dwell; but it is so much better to cherish happy thoughts and affectionate feelings. We should not concern ourselves about matters that do not need our attention. We should not concern ourselves as to what effect a drink of water will have; it is our business to drink it. We should not concern ourselves as to whether a grain of corn will come up or not, our business is to plant it. It is our business to reach by example as well as precent. Every where in the Bible there are numerous evidences that God Almighty calls and sanctifies men to go and do his will; and the man who occupies the ministry merely as a profession, and seeks it for its honors, (for a great many people think there are a wonderful sight of honors associated with it) if they knew as much about it as I do, they would not have fanciful ideas. O! what a responsible calling it is, to go out to help the Lord of hosts—to go out to speak for the God of the universe—to go out and snatch men from the precipice or brink of eternal ruin as the old time preachers use to say, "hell hung and breeze shaken, and to go out to save men from ruin's brink. The man who does not go out in harmony with God and his word is out of his place as a minister.

There were plenty of prophets in the days of Jeremiah as the country was flooded with them, who professed to be reliable, and tried to discredit Jeremiah. They said he was behind the age, and could not be depended upon. In their pride and pomposity, they said, are we not the house of Abraham? Did not God bring us out of Egyptian bondage? Did he not divide the very sea for us? Did he not sustain our fathers on manna? Did he not take care even of the clothes we wore that lasted during the forty years we were in the wilderness? Did not he strike the very rock itself—and it became a river of living water? and now you talk about the king of Babylon coming up here to capture us after God swearing to Abraham, Isaac and Jacob that we should be a great nation. The idea of destroying the temple and leading us into captivity is all nonsense. But then there was a venerable man of God whose counsels were rejected, who was hated and despised, lifting up his voice against the popular sins, telling backsliding Israel, if you repent, you will have pastors after God's own heart. He promised them instruction that would give the people knowledge, and that knowledge should not be alone; he will give you that which is more than knowledge. A man may have knowledge, and still be a fool. He may be schooled in books without understanding, without the wisdom, philosophy, the application and utilization of knowledge. It sometimes happens that persons have just enough knowledge to embarrass others without it being any benefit to themselves. I remember a good many years ago that there was a man in Washington city who belonged to my congregation, who was considered a good scholar, and who was hypocritical in matters of grammer. It was his disposition to criticize every public speaker or preacher that he heard. At that time my education was rather imperfect, and I did not have as much knowledge of the English language as I have now. I was not very choice in my diction, and I was conscious of many errors. As I stood up and tried to preach, the perspiration flowed freely. I labored as I hardly labored before, in order to escape the condemnation of that miserable critic. I never shall forget the circumstance. Bishop Brown remembers when I was at Israel church. The next Sunday after my unpleasant experience in preaching in the presence of the critic, I went into my study, got on my knees and promised God, grammer or no grammer, that I intended to preach God's eternal word as best I could. I then preached, and I did not know that the miserable fellow was there; and on that occasion, God added a convert to the church. I moved on in the same line and many were converted, the debts of the church were paid, prosperity spread its wings over the work, and God honored us with a glorious year. My brethren, do you want to be pastors after God's own heart? What does this require you to do? If you will take my advice to-day, you will read the scriptures. You want to know more than that. You want to know that you are born of God. You want the company of the holy spirit. You want to feel your preaching. Whenever you are in a condition that you do not feel the weight of souls, and are not willing to make sacrifices and work for souls, you may know there is something wrong with you.

But you should have knowledge. I want you distinctly to understand that I make no reflection on knowledge. You should have a knowledge of letters, a knowledge of science, a knowledge of history, a knowledge of the classics and a knowledge of everything possible for you to obtain. There are scores of things you will never be able to fully understand until you can read the holy scriptures in the original languages. If you would go to the bottom of certain passages, you would know well to study the Hebrew and the Greek. I know whereof I speak. You need to study the rocks, the trees, the flowers, the rivers, the mountains, the birds, the beasts, and everything possible in nature. You want to know something of history, ancient as well as modern—the rise and downfall of empires, and all else that transpired. You have got a head big enough to contain it all. It is all nonsense to talk about men not having a general knowledge of the universe. A man has twenty-eight million brain fibers. You possess larger comprehensions than you often imagine. You do not know the power you possess. While you need to develop your mind, you want that acquaintance with God, that communion with heaven and that application with the holy spirit that will teach you to lead the people in the right paths. In the gift of understanding, how stands the case with you to-day? Some of you older brethren will not aspire much in that direction. I want to say another thing. To be God's pastors is to be industrious. No lazy, sleepy nor inactive preacher is ever going to succeed in preaching the gospel. A preacher who sits about gossiping when he ought to be reading will never possess knowledge and understanding. You know there are many of our people who have no conception of study. They do not feel the need of it for themselves, nor sympathize with the effort of others. It sometimes happens that there are persons and places where I would visit, if I were certain of having a place where I could read and write. I am sometimes put into a room where I have neither a lamp or a table, or quiet even to think. The good people talk to me all the time, and invite all their friends and neighbors to assist them. The idea of asking a Bishop to stop at a place, with as many letters as we receive and as many as we expect to answer—and we cannot answer one in twenty—with no convenience, is rather unfortunate.

There will be times when it will be for you to take your books and go out in the woods and go up and down the road studying nature. You will do well to commit the scriptures to memory or as much as possible; but above all, my brethren, keep the Holy Spirit in you. Always aim to advance. Do not be satisfied with simply holding your own in the church. It is not enough to hold your own. You should increase, enlarge and leave the church stronger and in more favorable condition than when you took charge. A great many preachers fall because their hearts are not in the work. Some persons come into the ministry because they are too lazy to work; and they finally come to the conclusion that they will go to preaching. Such men never succeed. If you would be ministers of the Lord Jesus, be studious and devoted, and if your heart is in the work, you will succeed. You need never be afraid of overexerting yourself. It is all nonsense to talk about working yourself to death by preaching the gospel. . . . The more you preach, the longer you will live. . . . I have talked longer than I intended. God bless you, my brethren, God sanctify you, and God save you is my prayer.

Bishop H. M. Turner's Address before New Jersey Conference

Delivered at the New Jersey Annual Conference of the African
Methodist Episcopal Church, Asbury Park, ca. April 29, 1891

SOURCE: *Christian Recorder*, May 7, 1891

*In this address, Turner focused his ire on the "lazy preacher," challenging the
ministers under his charge to attend to their responsibilities and to avoid
becoming "don't care minister[s]."*

Members of the New Jersey Annual Conference: After another year of separation and trial we meet in the name of the Great Head of the Church to
discharge such duties as are incumbent upon us. I hope our deportment
here will be in every respect in keeping with the majesty of our vocation.
It is to be presumed that our reports will be honestly and truthfully made.
I trust, however, that such points as may have been attended with some
hardship will not be pessimistically colored and thus strike terror to your
successor, if you should fail to be returned to the same work. For hundreds
of our ministers are no longer looking for places where they can do the most
good, but are chiefly concerned about what is commonly denominated good
appointments. Jesus Christ, who was a philosopher as well as the Son of God
and the Saviour of the world, said when he was upon the earth in the flesh,

"He that is unfaithful in that which is little will be unfaithful over much."[1] Christ meant that a minister who would not take care of a small charge will not take care of a large one. And my observations for over thirty years have confirmed the truth of the Saviour's declaration.

I hope we will deal with each other in candor. If a brother needs a little pruning or even an excoriation let it be administered with all the severity necessary, but let us not forget that Jesus says, "Blessed are the merciful, for they shall obtain mercy."[2] Kill no brother that you can save; let kindness permeate all you dealing with a brother who has even been unfortunate; yet there is one class that neither God nor nature has any sympathy with. I mean the laggard.

Nature, it is said, abhors a vacuum. God and nature abhors laziness. No lazy preacher should be kept in the itinerant ranks. True, it may not be his fault; it may be due to the condition of his parents at his conception, but nevertheless, in the language of Bishop Payne: "It is his misfortune." Our church has suffered more of late years at the hands of lazy pastors than all the other complaints aggregated against our ministry. I could instance fifty things, but will only mention one in this connection, and that one is the common disuse of love feast tickets. Why have love feast tickets almost become a strange thing in our Church? The answer is that the preachers have been too lazy to get the tickets, sign their names to them and see that the leaders distributed them among the members, or distribute them themselves. Yet these tickets would bring thousands of dollars into our Church yearly and thousands of dollars, too, for the support of the very men who are too unpardonably lazy to prepare the tickets and see that they are distributed among the members. But no, they had rather preach a miserable, dead sermon, void of all vitality or inspiration and then set out the table.

Table collections for everything have become a nuisance in our Church. Would to God I could see the day when table collections could be dispensed with or reserved for extraordinary occasions. The minister who will rise up and inaugurate some other plan for collecting money and inspire the Church with its wisdom and importance will be a Connectional Benefactor and I would vote to make him Arch-Bishop. But laziness and slovenliness go hand-in-hand, and wherever they are found in a minister and his presiding

---

1. Luke 16:10.
2. Matthew 5:7.

elder does not move for his location, the presiding elder is not true to his Church, his God or his conscience. I ask no mercy at your hands for the lazy, sloven and don't-care minister, for there is nothing in him and never will be. Industry, particularity, attention to business, to rule and order must be born in a man. You can never preach them in him, advise them in him, threaten them in him or coax them in him. The lazy preacher is doomed "World without end."

Bishop Turner's Opening Address before the Philadelphia Conference

Delivered at the Philadelphia Conference of the African Methodist Episcopal Church, Bethel Church, West Chester, Pennsylvania, May 13, 1891

SOURCE: *Christian Recorder*, May 21, 1891

Here, Turner defended his fellow bishops against the charge that they only celebrated pastors who raised a lot of money. Turner called for a more spiritual church, arguing that it would inspire donor generosity toward the church and its ministers.

Members of the Philadelphia Annual Conference.

In the providence of God we have been enabled to run the circuit of another year. Many changes have taken place since we last met. At least fifty million human beings have left the arena of an earthly existence and have gone to swell the number of the dead. Yet out of that vast number how few have fallen out of our ranks....

Since we met last the forces of nature have not been idle. Not only has the earth traveled two hundred and eighty millions of miles in its orbit with at least fifteen hundred million inhabitants upon its surface, but the sun, the luminous god of day, has walked through space, at least five millions of miles, and dragged over a hundred worlds in his wake. Oceans, rivers, winds, cold and heat and ten thousand other agencies in the hand of God, have played their part and unerringly executed the behests of heaven.

But how well you and I have discharged our duties will somewhat be determined by the reports we make during the session of this conference. Especially will this be indicated by the number of accessions to the church we may report; for, after all, my brethren, Heaven rates and values a minister in proportion to the souls he is instrumental in adding to the militant church. Money is an instrumental factor in the running machinery in the church of God, especially in this age when so few are willing to make sacrifices for the cause of the Redeemer.

But the minister who is a mere financier is no more to be compared to the soul-saving preacher, than earth is to be compared to heaven.

The church of God is older than money and it will be here when money corrodes and disappears. For money at best is only a temporary medium. It will not last always, but the Church of God is unending.

I have been told repeatedly, "you bishops do not care anything about a man unless he is a big money raiser." I pronounce the charge untrue. True, the man who is a successful financier,—with all other things equal—adds to his high vocation. But if it was made a square issue between soul saving and money raising, I do not believe there is a bishop in the church, but what would concede to the soul saver, double, yes, quintuple honor.

But I do not see why a God called minister cannot succeed in both.

The more a church is spiritualized the more liberal the people will be. I can take a spiritualized church and raise three times as much money from it as any man can from a dead formal congregation. The more people are taught to respect and reverence God, the more liberal they will be towards anything that God enjoins.

I beg to congratulate you upon the general increase of the work. Revivals have been abundant; new preaching points have been established; and a general enlargement of the work has been conspicuously manifested.

How much is due to the presiding elder system, I am not able to determine. That much of it is due to the establishment of the system, and the ability of its incumbents, is beyond doubt. I tried to give you first class ministers for presiding elders, and I think I succeeded tolerably well. No old broken down ministerial hag should ever be made a presiding elder. Any bishop who will take a man and make a presiding elder of him, who cannot succeed as a pastor, commits a great blunder. Indeed, no man has the qualifications for a presiding elder, who could not make a respectable bishop. In a few instances, I have made presiding elders out of men that the preachers virtually had to carry, but I shall never do it again knowingly. That is one reason why so many object to the presiding elder system. We bishops, in too many instances, have taken ministerial failures who should have been located and made presiding elders out of them, merely to provide a living for them at the expense of the church of God, and thousands who would have been brought to Christ had living men been put in the position.

Another thing, if you will indulge me, when you know that certain ministers are dead failures; why do you not locate them; or if they are old and worn out superannuate they? Why keep this worthless lumber on your hands when you know it serves no purpose, that brings any profit to the Church of God? When men will not study or cannot study (for some cannot) they cannot preach. Churches die on their hand and they are failures everywhere they go. You owe it to yourselves, to your church and to your God to locate them or superannuate them. Our Book of Discipline makes ample provision for disposing of men who are non-effective and yet leaves them in an honorable situation. It is no disgrace to be a local preacher; many of them have been great blessings to the Church of God, and to superannuate a minister by virtue of great work done and results accomplished and make him a pensioner upon the Church is an evidence of the highest respect. And the minister thus honored cannot feel that he has been reflected upon by his brethren. To be a traveling minister presupposes activity, vim, ability and reasonable health. Yet I would not advise you to be cruel, unreasonable, or to exhibit a spirit of intolerance toward those, especially who were building up the Church before two-thirds of you were born; for without fathers there can be no sons. . . .

I hope our deportment while here in the conference session will be in every respect harmonious with our exalted profession. Let each minister not forget to observe family prayer in whatever house he may lodge. I do not mean to merely say some little, old, dried, stereotyped prayer, but read, sing and pray. Should it be inconvenient to read the Bible it will not be inconvenient to sing a few verses before prayer anywhere. Every kind of public worship, either in the church or around the family altar, should be preceded with singing. I do not believe God ever called a man to preach who could not sing. This much I do know, however, that song, prayer and Christianity are inseparable.

I hope, brethren, that your sermons and addresses before the conference will not merely be intellectual feats, but will be such spiritual applications of divine truth as will aim to reach the hearts of the people. Intellectual preaching may be ornate or partake of the rhetorical embellishments, but it will not reach the souls of men unless it is saturated by the Holy Spirit.

Our annual conferences should be times of refreshing from the presence of the Lord. Our more aged and stronger ministers should imbue the younger and weaker with a higher sense of their calling, and set them examples of such affective preaching as God enjoins upon them.

I have heard it said, "Annual conferences are no place for revival work; wait till you go to your churches and get prepared for it." I would like to know if there is moment between the time that a man is called to preach and the grave when he should not be prepared for revival work. I would rather hear an ass bray than to listen at all the babble of such stupid men. . . .

Bishop H. M. Turner's Address before the New York Conference

Delivered at the New York Annual Conference of the African
Methodist Episcopal Church, Union Bethel Church, Brooklyn, New
York, May 27, 1891

SOURCE: *Christian Recorder*, June 4, 1891

*Speaking before the New York Conference, Turner discussed bishops' duties
and offered insight and wisdom regarding how to handle problems that arose.*

Members of the New York annual conference:—

After running through the gamut of life's duties for another year we meet
again under the most favorable auspices.

The benedictions of heaven have followed us, and notwithstanding some
have fallen out of our ranks by the chilly touch of death, a large majority are
here prepared to answer to roll call.

In the language of the poet, we have had "fightings without and fears within,"[1]
but the Lord has been the shield and buckler of all who put their trust in him.

I trust our conference deliberations will be in every particular congruous
with our exalted station.

---

1. Charles Wesley, "And Are We Yet Alive," https://hymnary.org/text/and_are_we_yet_alive.

You all know that I recognize no big and little men when we meet in conference. Every man is an equal upon the conference floor and every man is entitled to his say, provided it is not absolute waste of time by a repetition of the same words and a capitulation of the same ideas.

After the Philadelphia conference had concluded its business and adjourned, a certain brother approached me in the cars and began a long narrative about the condition of a certain church. I asked him why he did not state it before the conference? He replied by saying, that "His presiding elder would not let him talk before the conference." I told him he was foolish, and I would hear nothing he had to say about it. the idea of a full member of the conference sitting down six consecutive days and failing to represent an important matter in our conference because his presiding elder objected to it, proves to a demonstration that he is not fit to lead a lilliputian much less the members of the church of God. I am a presiding elder man. It is foolish to talk about running our church without them any longer, but any man who has sense enough to be a member of an annual conference, has sense enough to know that we are all equals on the conference floor.

Otherwise the presiding elder would be a Negro driver instead of a brother in Christ.

Whatever variableness may exist between us during the conference year, or whatever difference in point of capacity or ability may exist in respect to our individualities, disappears before the rights and privileges which every member possesses upon the conference floor.

I expect a number of you will not feel just as pleasant toward me as you otherwise would had it been in my power to visit you; for I told a number of you if Providence permitted, I would visit your churches this conference year and endeavor to encourage your members. But I have failed to do so in the main, and why? Solely because I could not. I do not believe that there is a lazy bone in my body, though I say it myself. But the hundreds and thousands of letters which pour in upon me, not alone from my Episcopal district, but from all parts of the country, is enough to occupy the absolute time and attention of any man on earth. Think of ten and fifteen letters a day coming in upon you and everyone expecting an answer. . . . I cannot believe that the other bishops are annoyed as I am with communications. If they are they ought to be released from all visitations and required to remain at home and correspond with the country. At the rate our bishops are bored with communications from the ministry, from newspaper editors, from authors for a review of their books, from church statisticians, for the numerical strength of our ministry, our members, our churches, our parsonages and forty other things about our Church and from office-seekers requesting recommendations to the President for positions of honor and trust with scores of other things, I repeat with these demands upon the bishops, they ought to be released from all Episcopal visitation and supplied with secretaries to keep up with the correspondence demanded. I have to employ secretaries and pay them out of my allowance; besides the vast amount of paper, envelopes and stamps must come out of the same allowance. I hear that some little souls are talking about cutting down the Bishops' salaries; they had better be talking about adding seven or eight hundred dollars more to it if they expect us to do the work demanded by the times and responsibilities. From May 1890 until May 1891 my correspondence has cost me $268, two hundred and sixty-eight dollars. Men forget our Church is growing and a bishop's responsibility is twenty times what it was twenty years ago. It is no uncommon thing for me to preach and sit up and write the balance of the night and take the cars next morning and sit and nod till the next point of destination and repeat the same act the following night. But I have covenanted with myself to stop it if I should see the end of this quadrennium.

Pardon me if I should refer to a very sensitive question. I call it sensitive because it is one of those questions which is required to be touched very tenderly. I find there is a great deal of electioneering going on as to who shall be chosen as bishops at our next General Conference and what the increase of bishops shall be.

I received a letter a few days ago from Mississippi numerously signed by influential persons presenting the name of Rev. Jas Porter[2] as a fit and worthy man to be elected a bishop at our next General Conference and requesting me to have Dr. Lee[3] publish the communication in the RECORDER. Grand, scholarly and successful as Brother Porter is, I shall not comply with the request. I positively believe that bishops should be voted for by the influence which comes from patient and protracted prayer. Nor should any man vote

---

2. James Ward Porter (ca. 1822–95) was an AME minister and a conductor on the Underground Railroad. In 1868, he joined Turner as one of Georgia's first Black state legislators.

3. Benjamin F. Lee (1841–1926) was an educator and president of Wilberforce University (1876–84). He also served as the editor of the *Christian Recorder* (1884–92) and was elected bishop in 1892.

to make another a bishop through personal considerations. In other words, merely because he likes him, nor even through sectional combinations. If a man is regarded as possessing the elements and characteristics which should blend into a bishop, let him be supported because of his individual merits. Nor do I see the necessity of trying to degrade one man to elevate another. Every person should vote for his choice without trying to asperse and vilify somebody else[.] I see no reason why I should pronounce A, mean and degraded because I am working for the election of B. I never expect to curse one man for the purpose of blessing another. Such a course is monstrously wicked, but the better plan, my brethren, is to talk about the grander phases of each other's worth and submit our votes to divine impressions. But I have not said what I started out to say. Here is what I want to say. Inasmuch as the election of one or two more bishops is under contemplation would it not be better for one or two friends of each prominent candidate to sit down and write a sketch of the life and services of their choice and show what this or that brother has done, what his attainments are, what his peculiar fitness is, what his special gifts are and lucidly set forth his virtues and publish the same in pamphlet form and scatter them broadcast among the delegates and let other candidates alone, and not be trying to show up the worthlessness and unfitness of one man for the position to help popularize another? I know that men will work and electioneer for the candidate of their choice. But as I said before, why try to curse one man to bless another? That thing ought to be stopped, and we colored people are the most addicted to it.

Our church however has reached such grand proportions, and we have such an exalted stock of eminent men to glean from, that it appears to me, we should rise to a higher plain in our electioneering efforts. . . .

I hope the presiding elders will present no man for admission into the conference who has not procured the books and mastered the course of study required for admission. The bishops at their council in Jacksonville, Fla., unanimously agreed to enforce the provisions of the law bearing upon the course of studies. The course of study is very cheap; the number of books have been diminished, and they are simple enough for any fifteen year old boy to master; and any preacher who is too worthless to procure them, is too worthless to make a pastor for our churches. And any presiding elder who will bring men for admission into conference who have not procured the prerequisite course of study, is unworthy of his exalted station. And I now say to the committee on admissions, I hope you will recommend no man who has not at least purchased and read, "Burder's Village Sermons."[4] It is a decent body of Divinity in itself. If candidates have not read some systematic Theology they will find the cardinal principles of it in these "Village Sermons."

Do you know that our conferences are being crowded with inferior men of late years?

Do you know that the appointing powers are burdened to death nearly, with how to dispose of this host of second and third class men?

Twenty, twenty-five and thirty years ago the majority of men admitted into our conferences had vim, snap and force about them, while they did not have as much education or learning as a common rule, a reasonable majority had native force and a stirring get up, were willing to make any sacrifice to serve the church and honor God[.] But it seems here of late, that a majority of those received are just to the reverse. You will admit a man into the conference to day, and in many instances if you appoint him to a work to-morrow, he will stop and look you in the face and ask you how many members are there; and what support he can get; and set up a grumble,—a thing that would have thrown a whole annual conference into a frenzy twenty or thirty years ago.

I remember the time when Bishops Quinn,[5] Payne, Nazery[6] and Campbell would have driven such men out of the house. The fathers would have sprung to their feet by scores and called for ropes.

I do not charge this upon all the young men coming into our conferences, but I do say, that the doors of admission into our itinerant work stand too much ajar. The sooner we lock the doors and require young men to furnish the key of merit, the better it will be for the future church.

The most rigid conference on that line, the church has ever had, was possibly the Baltimore conference. I remember well when committees would examine their candidates for admission, deacons and elders' orders, three hours a day for three and four consecutive days, and frequently would keep the candidates before them all night long. I have known committees to meet at ten o'clock in the night, and examine candidates till six o'clock next morning; and what followed? Why the Baltimore conference has given the church more famous ministers than any conference in the connection. In many instances they required the candidates to bring their books into the

---

4. George Burder, *Village Sermons; or, One Hundred and One Plain and Short Discourses on the Principal Doctrines of the Gospel* (Philadelphia: Lippincott, 1860).

5. William Paul Quinn (1788–1873) was a bishop in the AME Church.

6. Willis Nazery (1803–1875) was a bishop of the AME Church.

committee rooms, so that the committee might examine the books, and see to what extent the books had been used. Whether or not the books showed the impress of their finger marks. It will pay the conference to be rigorous in exacting a full compliance with the course so cheap and simple. Dereliction of duty in this direction will be treachery to the church of God, and the sequel will be ignorance, stupidity, non-progression, and an unexceptable ministry. As Jesus said "Pray therefore the Lord of the harvest, that he will send forth laborers into his harvest,"[7] such laborers as will meet the endorsement of heaven. . . .

You have doubtless been apprised of the fact that I have been designated by the late session of our Episcopal Council to visit Africa and see after our mission work there. I trust it will be the order of Providence to grant me this favor, for the chief of all my desires is to visit that the grandest of Continents. I hope you will pray that no calamity or misfortune may prevent the contemplated trip. I expected to start in July or August, but those who are acquainted with the meteorological conditions of Africa, or I might have said, African meteorography, advise me to wait until October. Dr. Coppin[8] promised to accompany me, but it is rather doubtful now whether he can go or not. Africa must be brought to God and I believe we are to be the chief agents in the consummation of the work. Moreover, you can ridicule it if you like, but Africa will be the thermometer that will determine the status of the Negro the world over.

We may boast of our American citizenship and that we are a part and parcel of this sham of a nation. But mark my words, the Negro will never be anything here while Africa is shrouded in heathen darkness. The elevation of the Negro in this and all other countries is indissolubly connected with the enlightenment of Africa; and this African church of which you and I are members, has sufficient culture in it to awaken to a realization of that fact. . . .

God grant us a pleasant session is my prayer. A word or so more, please. I hope you will not only remember to observe family worship at your respective stopping places, but that your very conversation will proclaim your professions.

---

7. Luke 10:2.

8. Levi Jenkins Coppin (1848–1924) was an educator, missionary, editor of the *AME Review*, and bishop of the AME Church.

Negro Convention Speech

Delivered at the National Negro Convention, Cincinnati,
November 28, 1893

Source: *Voice of Missions*, December 1893

In this speech, Turner highlighted the abuses that African Americans faced in the United States and argued that this oppression meant that Black people should "seek other quarters."

Gentlemen of the National Council

In pursuance of a call issued September 30th by the solicitation and endorsement of over 300 prominent and distinguished members of our race from every section of the United States we have assembled in a National Council today. The circumstances which bring us together all of the most grave, serious, and solemn character that could ever command attention and sober consideration. Our anomalous condition as a race, and the increasing evils under which we exist, have been impressing [on] me for the last four years that a National Convention or council of our people should assemble and speak to the country, at least, or sue in some other respects for better conditions. But as no one else appeared to be moving for the assembling of such a body your humble servant on the 18th of last July published through the papers an intention of calling such a council, provided it met the approval of any considerable number of the prominent colored men of the country. . . .

Let us, by way of premises, itemize a few facts connected with our career in this country. We have been inhabitants of this continent for 273 years, and a very limited part of that time were we citizens—I mean from the ratification of the XIV amendment of the national constitution until the Supreme Court of the United States, Oct. 15th, 1883, declared that provision of the constitution null and void, and decitizenized us.[1] Now, what does history set forth relative to our conduct and behavior during this our long residence?

While it is true that we were brought here as captive heathens, through the greed and avarice of the white man, to serve him as a slave, I believe that as over-ruling Providence suffered it to be because there was a great and grand purpose to be subserved, and that infinite wisdom intended to evolve ultimate good out of a temporary evil, and that in the ages to come, the glory of God will be made manifest and that millions will thank heaven for the limited toleration of American slavery. All of you may not accept my sentiments upon this point, but I believe there is a God, and that he takes cognizance of human events; for such a stupendous evil could not have existed so long, affecting the destiny of the unborn, without a glorious purpose in view.

However, since our forced introduction into this land, willingly or unwillingly, mankind will accord to us a fidelity to every interest that will command the respect of the world forever. As slaves, in the aggregate, we were obedient, faithful, and industrious. We felled the forests, tilled the ground, pioneered civilization and were harmless. Yet this same Goddess of Liberty has been transformed into a lying strumpet, so far as she symbolizes the civil liberties of the black man. . . .

The mule and forty acres of land, which has been so often ridiculed for being expected by the black man, was a just and righteous expectation, and had this nation been one-fiftieth part as loyal to the black man as he has been to it, such a bestowment would have been made, and the cost would have been a mere bagatelle, compared with the infinite resources of this Republic, which has given countless millions to foreigners to come into the country and destroy respect for the Sabbath, flood the land with every vice known

---

1. In 1883, the US Supreme Court ruled the 1875 Civil Rights Act unconstitutional. For more on Turner and the Supreme Court, see Andre E. Johnson, *No Future in This Country: The Prophetic Pessimism of Bishop Henry McNeal Turner* (Jackson: University Press of Mississippi, 2020), chapter 1.

to the ends of the earth, and form themselves into anarchial bands for the overthrow of its institutions, and venerated customs.

Nevertheless, freedom had been so long held up before us as man's normal birthright, and as the bas-relief of every possibility belonging to the achievements of manhood, that we received it as heaven's greatest boon and nursed ourselves into satisfaction, believing that we had the stamina, not only to wring existence out of our poverty, but also wealth, learning, honor, fame, and immortality. But through some satanic legerdemain, within the last three or four years, the most fearful crimes have been charged upon members of our race, known to the catalogue of villainy, and death and destruction have stalked abroad with an insatiable carnivoracity, that not only beggars description, but jeopardizes the life of every Negro in the land—as anyone could raise an alarm by crying rape, and some colored man must die, whether he is the right one or not, or whether it was the product of revenge or the mere cracking of a joke. . . .

Almost every day the very lightning of heaven is made to flash these horrible deeds from one end of the continent to the other; the allegations being that we are outraging and raping white women to such an extent that an editor of the *Christian Advocate* proclaims to the world that "three hundred white women have been raped by Negroes within the preceding three months." In other words, a high ecclesiastical representative charge that the members of our race are perpetrating a hundred rapes month upon the white women of the country. Another public daily paper tells the civilized world that Negroes raped seven hundred white women from the first day of last January up to October 10th, which is undoubtedly the most revolting and blood-curdling charge ever presented against a people since time began. Without, however, attempting to number the white women that black men have been charged with outraging, it is known to all present that not a week, and at times scarcely a day, has passed in the last three or four years but what some colored man has been hung, shot, or burned by mobs of lynchers, and justified or excused upon the plea that they had outraged some white married or single woman, or some little girl going to or from school. These crimes alleged against us, whether true or false, have been proclaimed by the newspapers of the country in such horrific terms that it would seem like an amazing grace that has held back the curse of God and the vengeance of man, to enable us to meet here today. For if the accusations are even half true, we must be allied to a race of such incarnate fiends that no hopeful prospect illumines our future. . . .

But gentlemen of the convention, there is another side to this question. Under the genius and theory of civilization throughout the world, no man is guilty of any crime, whatever, until he is arrested, tried by an impartial process of law, and deliberately convicted.... [A] mob can band themselves together and hang a Negro about perpetrating a rape upon some white woman, but rarely give the name of the individual, and when you visit the community and inquire as to who it was thus outraged, in many instances, nobody knows, and the mob is justified upon the plea that the Negro confessed it. Confessed it to whom? Confessed it to a set of bloody-handed murderers, just as though a set of men who were cruel enough to take the life of another were too moral to tell a lie. Strange, too, that the men who constitute these banditti can never be identified by the respective governors or the law officers, but the newspapers know all about them—can advance what they are going to do, how and when it was done, how the rope broke, how many balls entered the Negro's body, how loud he prayed, how piteously he begged, what he said, how long he was left hanging, how many composed the mob, the number that were masked, whether they were prominent citizens or not, how the fire was built that burnt the raper, how the Negro was tied, how he was thrown into the fire, and the whole transaction; but still the fiendish work was done by a set of "unknown men."

I fear that what I have been told in confidence by prominent white men, that a large number of associations are in existence, bound by solemn oaths and pledged to secrecy by the most binding covenants, to exterminate the Negro by utilizing every possible opportunity, has more truth in it than I was at first inclined to believe. For the white people all over the country have everything in their own hands, can do absolutely as they please in administering their own created laws to the Negro. They have all the judges, and all the juries, and virtually all the lawyers, all the jails, all the penitentiaries, all the ropes, all the powder, and all the guns; at least they manufacture them all, and why these hasty, illegal executions unless Negro extermination is the object desired? They evidently must fear a public trial, otherwise it is very singular that they should be so anxious to silence the tongue and close the lips of the only one who can speak in his own defense by putting him to death so hastily and without judge or jury. The white people of this country, almost without exception, claim to be constitutionally superior to the black man. Then why should a race so superior and so numerically, financially, and intellectually in advance of the colored man be so afraid of a raping wretch that they will not allow him a chance to open his inferior lips in his own defense? . . .

And unless this nation, North and South, East, and West, awakes from its slumbers and calls a halt to the reign of blood and carnage in this land, its dissolution and utter extermination is only a question of a short time. . . . The Negro is very small item in the body politic of this country, but his groans, prayers and innocent blood will speak to God day and night, and the God of the poor and helpless will come to his relief sooner or later, and another fratricidal war will be the sequence, though it may grow out of an issue as far from the Negro as midday is from midnight. For this is either a nation or a travesty. If it is a nation, every man East and West, North, and South, is bound to the protection of human life and the institutions of the country; but if it is a burlesque or a national sham, then the world ought to know it. . . .

The truth is, the nation as such, has no disposition to give us manhood protection anyway. Congress had constitutional power to pursue a runaway slave by legislation into any state and punish the man who would dare conceal him, and the Supreme Court of the United States sustained its legislation as long as slavery existed. Now the same Supreme Court has the power to declare that the Negro has no civil rights under the general government that will protect his citizenship, and authorize the states to legislate upon and for us, as they may like; and they are passing special acts to degrade the Negro by authority of the said high tribunal, and Congress proposes no remedy by legislation or by such a constitutional amendment as will give us the status of citizenship in the nation that is presumed we are to love and to sacrifice our lives, if need be, in the defense of. Yet Congress can legislate for the protection of the fish in the sea and the seals that gambol in our waters, and obligate its mien, its money, its navy, its army and its flag to protect, but the 8,000,000 or 10,000,000 of its black men and women, made in the image of God, possessing $265,000,000 worth of taxable property, with all their culture, refinement in many cases, and noble bearing, must be turned off to become the prey of violence, and when we appeal to the general government for protection and recognition, Justice, so-called, drops her scales and says, away with you.

I am abused as no other man in this nation because I am an African emigrationist, and while we are not here assembled to consider that question, nor do I mention it at the present time to impose it upon you, but if the present condition of things is to continue, I had not only rather see my people in the heart of Africa, but in ice-bound, ice-covered, and ice-fettered Greenland. "Give me liberty or give me death!" Other American Negroes may sing—"My country 'tis of thee, / Sweet land of liberty, / Of thee we sing." But here is one Negro whose tongue grows palsied whenever he is invited to put music to these lines.

As one, I feel grateful for many things that have been done for us within the last 30 years. I am thankful for Mr. Lincoln's manumitting Proclamation, for its ratification by Congress, for the Thirteenth, Fourteenth and Fifteenth Amendments to the Constitution, which were placed there by the American people for the benefit of our race, even if the United States Supreme Court has destroyed the Fourteenth Amendment by its revolting decision.

I am thankful to our generous-hearted friends of the North, who have given voluntarily millions upon millions to aid in our education. I am thankful to the South for the school laws they have enacted and for the generous manner they have taxed themselves in building and sustaining schools for our enlightenment and intellectual and moral elevation.

But if this country is to be our home, the Negro must be a self-controlling, automatic factor of the body politic or collective life of the nation. In other words, we must be full-fledged men; otherwise, we will not be worth existence itself.

To passively remain here and occupy our present ignoble status, with the possibility of being shot, hung, or burnt, not only when we perpetrated deeds of violence ourselves, but whenever some bad white man wishes to black his face and outrage a female, as I am told is often done, is a matter of serious reflection. To do so would be to declare ourselves unfit to be free men or to assume the responsibilities which involve fatherhood and existence. For God hates the submission of cowardice. But on the other hand, to talk about physical resistance is literal madness. Nobody but an idiot would give it a moment's thought. The idea of eight or ten million of ex-slaves contending with sixty million people of the most powerful race under heaven! Think of two hundred and sixty-five millions of dollars battling with one hundred billions of dollars! Why we would not be a drop in the bucket. It is folly to indulge in such a thought for a moment. . . .

I know that thousands of our people hope and expect better times for the Negro in this country, but as one I see no signs of a reformation in our condition; to the contrary, we are being more and more degraded by legislative enactments and judicial decisions. Not a thing has been said or done that contemplates our elevation or the promotion of our manhood in twelve or fifteen years outside of promoting our education in erecting schools for our general enlightenment; but a hundred things have been done to crush out the last vestige of self-respect and to avalanche us with contempt. My remedy, without a change, is, as it would be folly to attempt resistance, and our appeals for better conditions are being unheeded, for that portion of us, at least, who feel we are self-reliant, to seek other quarters. . . .

We must agree upon some project. We must offer some plan of action to our people or admit that we are too ignorant and worthless to do anything. This nation justly, righteously, and divinely owes us for work and services rendered, billions of dollars, and if we cannot be treated as American people, we should ask for five hundred million dollars, at least, to begin an emigration somewhere, for it will cost, sooner or later, far more than that amount to keep the Negro down unless they re-establish slavery itself. Freedom and perpetual degradation are not in the economy of human events. It is against reason, against nature, against precedent and against God. A people who read, attend schools, receive the instruction of the pulpits, write for the public press, think, and furnish famous orators, cannot be chained to degradation forever. They will be a menace to the land, and God himself, with all the laws of nature, will help them fight the injustice, and no pomp or boast of heraldry prevent it, yet it may involve horror to both races. Money to leave and build up a nation of our own, where we can respect ourselves at least, or justice at the hands of the American nation, should be the watch word of every Negro in the land. . . .

You evidently see from the points I have endeavored to raise, and many more that I have not touched, that our condition in this country inferiorates us, and no amount of book-learning, divested of manhood, respect and manhood promptings will ever make us a great people; for, underlying all school culture, must exist the consciousness that I am somebody, that I am a man, that I am as much as anybody else, that I have rights, that I am a creature of law and order, that I am entitled to respect, that every avenue to distinction is mine. For where this consciousness does not form the substratum of any people, inferioration, retrogression and ultimate degradation will be the result. And seeing that this is our status in the United States today, it devolves upon us to project a remedy for our condition, if such a remedy is obtainable, or demand of this nation, which owes us billions of dollars for work done and services rendered, five hundred million dollars to commence leaving it; or endorse the petition of the colored lawyers' convention which was held in Chattanooga, Tenn., asking Congress for a billion dollars for the same purpose.

For I can prove, by mathematical calculation, that this country owes us forty billion dollars for daily work performed. The one great desideratum of the American Negro is manhood impetus. We may educate and acquire general intelligence, but our sons and daughters will come out of college with all their years of training and drift to the plane of the scullion as long as they are restricted, limited and circumscribed by colorphobia. For abstract education elevates no man, nor will it elevate a race. What we call the heathen African will strut around his native land, three-fourths naked, and you can see by the way he stands, talks, and acts, that he possesses more manhood than fifty of some of our people in this country, and any ten of our most distinguished colored men here; and until we are free from menace by lynchers, hotels, railroads, stores, factories, restaurants, barber shops, machine shops, court houses and other places, where merit and worth are respected, we are destined to be a dwarfed people. Our sons and daughters will grow up with it in their very flesh and bones.

Gentlemen of the National Council, I leave the grave, solemn, and awful subject with you.

The American Negro and His Fatherland

Delivered at the Congress on Africa, Gammon Theological Seminary, Atlanta, December 1895

Source: Henry McNeal Turner, "The American Negro and His Fatherland," in *Addresses and Proceedings of the Congress on Africa Held under the Auspices of the Stewart Missionary Foundation for Africa of Gammon Theological Seminary in Connection with the Cotton States and International Exposition, December 13–15, 1895,* edited by J. W. E. Bowen (Atlanta: Gammon Theological Seminary, 1896), 195–98

On this occasion, Turner argued that the great chasm between Blacks and whites in the United States led members of both groups to believe in the natural inferiority of African Americans and thus prevented them from using their intellectual acumen to build and produce in beneficial ways.

It would be a waste of time to expend much labor, the few moments I have to devote to this subject, upon the present status of the Negroid race in the United States. It is too well known already. However, I believe that the Negro was brought to this country in the providence of God to a heaven-permitted if not a divine-sanctioned manual laboring school, that he might have direct contact with the mightiest race that ever trod the face of the globe.

The heathen African, to my certain knowledge, I care not what others may say, eagerly yearn for that civilization which they believe will elevate them and make them potential for good. The African was not sent and brought to this country by chance, or by the avarice of the white man, single and alone. The white slave purchaser went to the shores of that continent and bought our ancestors from their African masters. The bulk who were brought to this country were the children of parents who had been in slavery a thousand years. Yet hereditary slavery is not universal among the African slave-holders. So that the argument often advanced, that the white man went to Africa and stole us, is not true. They bought us out of a slavery that still exists over a large portion of that continent. For there are millions and millions of slaves in Africa to-day. Thus, the superior African sent us, and the white man brought us, and we remained in slavery as long as it was necessary to learn that a God, who is a spirit, made the world and controls it, and that that Supreme Being could be sought and found by the exercise of faith in His only begotten Son. Slavery then went down, and the colored man was thrown upon his own responsibility, and here he is today, in the providence of God, cultivating self-reliance and imbibing a knowledge of civil law in contra-distinction to the dictum of one man, which was the law of the black man until slavery was overthrown. I believe that the Negroid race has been free long enough now to begin to think for himself and plan for better conditions than he can lay claim to in this country or ever will. *There is no manhood future in the United States for the Negro.* He may eke out an existence for generations to come, but he can never be a man—full, symmetrical and undwarfed. Upon this point I know thousands who make pretensions to scholarship, white and colored, will differ and may charge me with folly, while I in turn pity their ignorance of history and political and civil sociology. We beg here to itemize and give a cursory glance at a few facts calculated to convince any man who is not biased or lamentably ignorant. Let us note a few of them.

1. There is a great chasm between the white and black, not only in this country, but in the West India Islands, South America, and as much as has been said to the contrary, I have seen inklings of it in Ireland, in England, in France, in Germany, and even away down in southern Spain in sight of Morocco in Africa. We will not however deal with foreign nations, but let us note a few facts connected with the United States.

I repeat that a great chasm exists between the two race varieties in this country. The white people, neither North nor South, will have social contact as a mass between themselves and any portion of the Negroid race. Although they may be as white in appearance as themselves, yet a drop of African blood imparts a taint, and the talk about two races remaining in the same country with mutual interest and responsibility in its institutions and progress, with no social contact, is the jargon of folly, and no man who has read the history of nations and the development of countries, and the agencies which have culminated in the homogeneity of racial variations, will proclaim such a doctrine. Senator Morgan,[1] of Alabama, tells the truth when he says that the Negro has nothing to expect without social equality with the whites, and that the whites will never grant it.

This question must be examined and opinions reached in the light of history and sociological philosophy, and not by a mere think-so on the part of men devoid of learning. When I use the term learning, I do not refer to men who have graduated from some college and have a smattering knowledge of Greek, Latin, mathematics and a few schoolbooks, and have done nothing since but read the trashy articles of newspapers. That is not scholarship. Scholarship consists in wading through dusty volumes for forty and fifty years. That class of men would not dare to predict symmetrical manhood for the Negroid race in this or any other country, without social equality. The colored man who will stand up and in one breath say, that the Negroid race does not want social equality and in the next predict a great future in the face of all the proscription of which the colored man is the victim, is either an ignoramus, or is an advocate of the perpetual servility and degradation of his race variety. I know, as Senator Morgan says, and as every white man in the land will say, that the whites will not grant social equality to the Negroid race, nor am I certain that God wants them to do it. And as such, I believe that two or three millions of us should return to the land of our ancestors, and establish our own nation, civilization, laws, customs, style of manufacture, and not only give the world, like other race varieties, the benefit of our individuality, but build up social conditions peculiarly our own, and cease to be grumblers, chronic complainers and a menace to the white man's country, or the country he claims and is bound to dominate.

---

1. Former Confederate general John Tyler Morgan (1824–1907) represented Alabama in the US Senate from 1877 to 1907, during which time he advocated for the repeal of the Fifteenth Amendment and for additional legislation designed to maintain white power in the South.

The civil status of the Negro is simply what the white man grants of his own free will and accord. The black man can demand nothing. He is deposed from the jury and tried, convicted and sentenced by men who do not claim to be his peers. On the railroads, where the colored race is found in the largest numbers, he is the victim of proscription, and he must ride in the Jim Crow car or walk. The Supreme Court of the United States decided, October 15th, 1882 [1883], that the colored man had no civil rights under the general government, and the several States, from then until now, have been enacting laws which limit, curtail and deprive him of his civil rights, immunities and privileges, until he is now being disfranchised, and where it will end no one can divine. . . .

2. The environments of the Negroid race variety in this country tend to the inferiority of them, even if the argument can be established that we are equals with the white man in the aggregate, notwithstanding the same opportunities may be enjoyed in the schools. Let us note a few facts.

The discriminating laws, all will concede, are degrading to those against whom they operate, and the degrader will be degraded also. "For all acts are reactionary, and will return in curses upon those who curse," said Stephen A. Douglass [sic], the great competitor of President Lincoln. Neither does it require a philosopher to inform you that degradation begets degradation. Any people oppressed, proscribed, belied, slandered, burned, flayed and lynched will not only become cowardly and servile, but will transmit that same servility to their posterity, and continue to do so ad infinitum, and as such will never make a bold and courageous people. The condition of the Negro in the United States is so repugnant to the instincts of respected manhood that thousands, yea hundreds of thousands, of miscegenated will pass for white, and snub the people with whom they are identified at every opportunity, thus destroying themselves, or at least unracing themselves. They do not want to be black because of its ignoble condition, and they cannot be white, thus they become monstrosities. Thousands of young men who are even educated by white teachers never have any respect for people of their own color and spend their days as devotees of white gods. Hundreds, if not thousands, of the terms employed by the white race in the English language are also degrading to the black man. Everything that is satanic, corrupt, base and infamous is denominated black, and all that constitutes virtue, purity, innocence, religion, and that which is divine and heavenly, is represented as white. Our Sabbath-school children, by the time they reach proper consciousness, are taught to sing to the laudation of white and to the contempt of black. Can any one with an ounce of common sense expect that these children, when they reach maturity, will ever have any respect for their black or colored faces, or the faces of their associates? But, without multiplying words, the terms used in our religious experience, and the hymns we sing in many instances, are degrading, and will be as long as the black man is surrounded by the idea that *white* represents God and black represents the devil. The Negro should, therefore, build up a nation of his own, and create a language in keeping with his color, as the whites have done. Nor will he ever respect himself until he does it.

3. In this country the colored man, with a few honorable exceptions, folds his arms and waits for the white man to propose, project, erect, invent, discover, combine, plan and execute everything connected with civilization, including machinery, finance, and indeed everything. This, in the nature of things, dwarfs the colored man and allows his great faculties to slumber from the cradle to the grave. Yet he possesses mechanical and inventive genius, I believe, equal to any race on earth. Much has been said about the natural inability of the colored race to engage in the professions of skilled labor. Yet before the war, right here in this Southland, he erected and completed all of the fine edifices in which the lords of the land luxuriated. It is idle talk to speak of a colored man not being a success in skilled labor or the fine arts. What the black man needs is a country and surroundings in harmony with his color and with respect for his manhood. Upon this point I would delight to dwell longer if I had time. Thousands of white people in this country are ever and anon advising the colored people to keep out of politics, but they do not advise themselves. If the Negro is a man in keeping with other men, why should he be less concerned about politics than anyone else? Strange, too, that a number of would-be colored leaders are ignorant and debased enough to proclaim the same foolish jargon. For the Negro to stay out of politics is to level himself with a horse or a cow, which is no politician, and the Negro who does it proclaims his inability to take part in political affairs. If the Negro is to be a man, full and complete, he must take part in everything that belongs to manhood. If he omits a single duty, responsibility or privilege, to that extent he is limited and incomplete.

Time, however, forbids my continuing the discussion of this subject, roughly and hastily as these thoughts have been thrown together. Not being able to present a dozen or two more phases, which I would cheerfully and gladly do if opportunity permitted, I conclude by saying the argument that it would be impossible to transport the colored people of the United States back to Africa is an advertisement of folly. Two hundred millions of dollars would rid this country of the last member of the Negroid race, if such a thing was desirable, and two hundred and fifty millions would give every man, woman and child excellent fare, and the general government could furnish that amount and never miss it, and that would only be the pitiful sum of a million dollars a year for the time we labored for nothing, and for which somebody or some power is responsible.

Eulogy: James C. Embry

Delivered at the Bethel African Methodist Episcopal Church,
Philadelphia, August 16, 1897

SOURCE: *Southern Christian Recorder*, September 9, 1897

James C. Embry (1834–97) served as an AME bishop beginning in 1896 and is credited with writing the denomination's first systematic theology, The Digest of Christian Theology: Designed for the Use of Beginners in the Study of Theological Science *(Philadelphia: AME Book Concern, 1890).*[1] *Turner spoke on a passage from II Samuel 1:25, "How the mighty have fallen in the midst of battle."*

[Y]ou remember during the great battle between the house of Israel and the Philistines, the known enemies of God's people that the tide of battle turned against the kingdom of Israel.

Saul supported by his son Jonathan, heir to the throne and his successor. Saul retreating pursued by the Philistine host, and rather than fall victim to the vengeance of the idolatrous and ungod fearing people, put the sword to his own breast fell upon it and took his life.

---

1. Dennis C. Dickerson, *The African American Methodist Episcopal Church: A History* (New York: Cambridge University Press, 2020), 172.

One of the sons of Amaleck saw the sight and rushed to David with the news that Saul was destroyed, but Saul was defying the honor of heaven and the government of Israel; but still was true to his people. But the messenger reported that Saul was dead, and brought his crown etc., to David as evidence that he had rid him of his great enemy. But he lost his life by it; David asked him how dare you lay your hands upon God's anointed?. . . .

The words I have selected are a part of the many I might read here: "How are the mighty fallen."

I need not tell of the affection by David shown for Jonathan.

The affection between the two men, like that between a husband and a lovable wife. This express or manifest affection is brought out more with reference to Jonathan who had also fallen than to his father, Saul, though he recognized that Saul had been selected and assigned to the kingdom of Israel.

But the purpose of this passage is not that I might enter into any extensive explanation of the incidents and characters with which it stands related. But simply to dwell upon these words, "How are the mighty fallen," with relation to the subject before us.

The A.M.E. Church, and I may say the race, are in mourning to day at the loss of one of her most eminent and distinguished sons.

The death of James C. Embry is no family matter, though a matter of family consideration and family grief. Not only do his children lose a father, an affectionate father, an honorable father, supporter, adviser, and counsellor, but the church mourns his loss as hers, from one end of the land to the other and it will be taken up by the Isles of the Sea around three sides of the continent of Africa. When tidings of his death shall reach our scores of missionaries and members in distant lands they will join with us in regretting the loss of this man of God.

Bishop Arnett's[2] beautiful portrait showed some of the most prominent features of his life in sketch, I need not refer to them. Let me say brother Bishops and Ministers, I have never seen on any occasion so many ministers of the Gospel from all sections of the church as I find here to-day.

In the demise of Bishop Embry, this upright, faithful unwavering son of the church we part with one who laid flesh and blood aside as we lay aside our clothes by and retire to rest.

---

2. Benjamin W. Arnett (1838–1906) was elected bishop of the AME Church in 1888. He had previously served as the denomination's financial secretary and been active in the Colored Conventions movement.

His Education.

He was self-educated.

A man of burdens and crosses, remember he has had a hard life, the constant work and great affliction. I believe he has been married the third time, his last wife departing this life a few months ago and I have no doubt that the grief and anguish together with the labors and trials of the book rooms hastened the end now reached.

The publishing department is a place I am familiar with. I am surprised that he held up as well as he did for so many years staying there longer than any other did[.]

But he stayed there burdened with its debts, its burdens, its tears, with the treachery of his brethren, with loss of confidence, and criticism, compiling church service, hymn books, and grappling with the most powerful questions of Theology. Putting them into book form and after all making himself the greatest theologian of the church.

If he was not in fact the greatest theologian by virtue of deeper learning, wide reading and abundant knowledge and experience. If any body wants to dispute this in favor of anybody else, the fact that he did collect and give the church the grandest work of any, puts him in the front rank.

As a Man.

Bishop Embry was a man whose word was his bond. Of integrity of life and spotless character. No man could point to his life or any part of it and entertain any doubt as to it.

So his fidelity to his God and his church.

He came upon the deck of the ship of church just when such men were needed. . . .

Embry came along about that time. No college, no library at hand, nor open school doors to give our young men science.

He picked up what he did get from private teachers, studying Greek here and Hebrew, Latin and German there. He was a self-made man, and yet this self-made man has given us the ablest work on Christian theology. Then a condensed form of the hymn book and church service and some of the ablest productions that have ever come from any man of the church.

He was peculiarly fitted for the work of his church, and there was no department of the church over which he could not preside. I have no doubt, in his labors in the publication department and on the books he wrote, he kept pace with the times.

His General Information.

He was up on every question, on everything in fact; this hastened him to the tomb. But there is no affliction as far as he is concerned. Some men live longer in ten years than others do in forty. All depends upon the industry, application and noble purpose that actuate and engage them for the good of their fellow men.

Lesson to Our Young Men.

I have lived to be classed among the fathers of the church, and the word Senior Bishop is frequently used now. I take advantage of the respect done your humble servant to warn you, young men, that whatever respect you have for this great man sleeping before us, if you honor his memory, you must emulate his great and noble example. We want more books; not only hymn books, but others such as he wrote.

I am almost sick and tired of these graduates coming out of colleges and practically giving us nothing. Many afflicted with the "big head," who want to step into the first pulpits of the land. . . .

. . . I want to say to you of Bishop Embry, you can't blame no college for his literary defects. If he could play the part which he did play so well, filling such pulpits as he did, and come finally to be honored by his brethren as he is, and as he was as financial secretary and twelve years head of the publication department, writing appeals, editorials for the Christian Recorder, giving the church standard works upon theology, general conference, embracing the same in its curriculum of study for the ministry a work mighty in influence and power as an elevating factor of the race, and yet "a child of no college." I hope you young men may honor him by enlarging upon his works of theology. . . .

We need book writers. We need hymns written by the race; need historians that will walk through the labyrinth of historic lore and pick out and put together and hand down to our children, then will we witness grander results in coming days.

HIS RACE.

He loved his race, and that eloquent tongue and mighty pen were ever ready to defend it, even to the moment of his death. He was not only a rhetoritian, while he was chaste in his diction, he was at the same time logical, deep, philosophic.

True, there are a great many persons who are also to shine rhetorically and delight in glittering generalities, but when they stop there is very little found to have been gained by what they have said.

But the man who sat and listened to Bishop Embry went away freighted, loaded down.

I believe he was the greatest Bishop that we have ever had. I say so in the face of the great Bishops we have had, such as Payne and Campbell, Brown, . . . and Ward. . . .

We have never had a Bishop that could stand up and give us more sermon in one than he. In five minutes I have picked up five or six sermons from him. He gave me "germ thoughts."

In the death of this great man we may well ask the question "How has the mighty fallen in the midst of battle." Truly, we are in the midst of the battle, the condition of affairs touching us in this country is anomalies. We don't know where we are. Look at the legislation of this country, this nation; look at the position of the supreme court; look at the hordes of lynchers cursing this land every day, causing misery, wretchedness and blighted and broken homes.

Only God can see the future. It looks as though if we ever needed a man of such courage and principles, it is now. This man of eloquence, of power, of character, logical, analytical and of wonderful synthetical powers, powers to pick to pieces and get out the good and expose the wrong. . . .

It is just now, "in the midst of the battle," he has fallen.

Perhaps God has other use for him. God has millions, billions, trillions of worlds. It may be that such a man as he was needed to take charge of some of the principalities and powers of God.

So, after all, God doest right. And we pray that he may speak volumes to these young men who come to do honor to this fallen hero. Oh, that his richest blessings may rest upon the children, the tender loved ones, of this man of God.

God Is a Negro

SOURCE: *Voice of Missions,* February 1898

In response to Turner's declaration that "God is a Negro," the Charlotte
Observer *opined that "the good Bishop has been represented as one of the
ablest men of his race and we thought justly so, for he is not only an intelligent thinker, but upon all subjects connected with his people his reasoning is
profound and in most instances unanswerable, but he is evidently becoming
demented if he used the language attributed to him." Turner struck back with
an editorial of his own.*[1]

The *Observer* has our thanks for the compliment tendered in respect to our
thinking faculties, notwithstanding our demented condition when we understand God to be a Negro. We have as much right biblically and otherwise to
believe that God is a Negro, as you buckra, or white, people have to believe
that God is a fine looking, symmetrical and ornamented white man. For the
bulk of you, and all the fool Negroes of the country, believe that God is white-
skinned, blue-eyed, straight-haired, projecting-nosed compressed-lipped and
finely-robed white gentleman sitting upon a throne somewhere in the heavens.

1. For more on Turner's "God Is a Negro," see Andre E. Johnson, *No Future in This
Country: The Prophetic Pessimism of Bishop Henry McNeal Turner* (Jackson: University Press
of Mississippi, 2020), esp. chapter 2; Andre E. Johnson, "God Is a Negro: The (Rhetorical)
Black Theology of Bishop Henry McNeal Turner," *Black Theology* 13, no. 1 (April 2015):
29–40.

Every race of people since time began who have attempted to describe their God by words, or by paintings, or by carvings, or by any other form or figure have conveyed the idea that the God who made them and shaped their destinies was symbolized in themselves, and why should not the Negro believe that he resembles God as much as other people? We do not believe that there is any hope for a race of people who do not believe that they look like God.

Demented though we be, whenever we reach the conclusion that God or even that Jesus Christ, while in the flesh, was a white man, we shall hang our gospel trumpet upon the willow and cease to preach.

We had rather be an atheist and believe in no God or a pantheist and believe that all nature is God, than to believe in the personality of a God and not believe that He is Negro. Blackness is much older than whiteness, for black was here before white, if the Hebrew word, coshach, or chasack, has any meaning. We do not believe in the eternity of matter, but we do believe that chaos floated in infinite darkness or blackness, millions, billions, quintillions and eons of years before God said, "Let there be light," and that during that time God had no material light Himself and was shrouded in darkness, so far as human comprehension is able to grasp the situation.

Yet we are no stickler as to God's color, anyway, but if He has any we should prefer to believe that it is nearer symbolized in the blue sky above us and the blue water of the seas and oceans; but we certainly protest against God being a white man or against God being white at all; abstract as this theme must forever remain while we are in the flesh. This is one of the reasons we favor African emigration, or Negro nationalization, wherever we can find a domain, for as long as we remain among whites, the Negro will believe that the devil is black and that he (the Negro) favors the devil, and that God is white and that he (the Negro) bears no resemblance to Him, and the effect of such a sentiment is contemptuous and degrading, and one-half of the Negro race will be trying to get white and the other half will spend their days trying to be white men's scullions in order to please the whites; and the time they should be giving to the study of such things will dignify and make our race great will be devoted to studying about how unfortunate they are in not being white.

We conclude these remarks by repeating for the information of the *Observer* what it adjudged us demented for—God is a Negro.

A Speech in Support of William Jennings Bryan for President

Delivered in Chicago, September 1, 1900

SOURCE: *Valentine* (Nebraska) *Democrat*, September 27, 1900

William Jennings Bryan (1860–1925) was a Democratic member of the US House of Representatives from Nebraska (1891–95) and US presidential candidate in 1896, 1900, and 1908. He went on to serve as secretary of state under President Woodrow Wilson (1913–15).

I am declaring my preference for William Jennings Bryan for president because he represents the same broad principles that Abraham Lincoln espoused and I believe it will be for the benefit of my people to vote for him. As Abraham Lincoln was a friend to the colored race, so is William Jennings Bryan.

All of this silly sentiment of adhering to the republican party because of Lincoln's proclamation of emancipation is misapplied. The republican party of Lincoln and the republican party of Hanna[1] are distinctly things apart. Lincoln is dead, but his principles of personal liberty still live, and verily the

---

1. Mark Hanna (1837–1904) was a US Senator from Ohio (1897–1904) and the chair of the Republican National Committee (1896–1904).

mantle of Elijah never fitted the shoulders of Elisha[2] as perfectly as Lincoln's mantle fits the broad shoulders of Bryan.

Was Friend of People.

Lincoln never harbored a trust. He never believed in governing without the consent of the governed. He never believed in grinding down the rights and privileges of the common people. He never failed to accord honor where honor was due. Now how can anyone reconcile the party principles of Lincoln with the party principles of Hanna and Roosevelt?[3]

In its treatment of the colored man the republican party has always masqueraded as a wolf in sheep's clothing. Since the time that party claims to have freed the slaves its managers have constantly lied to the colored man. When Lincoln died, republican honesty to the colored race was interred with his bones, and an era of republican moral degeneracy began. We are told that we were emancipated for humanity's sake. Yes, and I believe Cuba, Porto Rico and the Philippine islands were freed from the same incentive. Oh, humanity, what crimes are committed in thy name!

The republicans have lied to us about our freedom and our citizenship. Our freedom was a war necessity, and was dearly bought with colored arms 200,000 strong, and our citizenship is a replica of serfdom.

After the war the republicans, seeking to retain themselves in power, inaugurated the journeyman government system in the south, which is not only a blot upon our national escutcheon, but the secret of all the American colored man's social troubles today. They thrust the unsuspecting negro's hands into the fire to snatch out their chestnuts.

No Mortgage on Vote.

Contrary to the emotional idea that the republican party has an unlimited mortgage on the suffrages of the colored man, I say that the organization

---

2. The story of Elisha receiving the mantle from Elijah is told in 2 Kings 2. Elisha was an apprentice of Elijah, and when Elijah died, a "double portion of his spirit" rested on Elisha.

3. Theodore Roosevelt (1858–1919) served as governor of New York (1899–1900), US vice president (March–September 1901), and US president (1901–9).

should be everlastingly grateful to the colored man. The republican party is the child of that race. Through Lincoln's honest championship of the enslaved people that party was born. Through the colored man's gratitude it was bred. The black man behind the gun turned the tide of the rebellion thus insuring the power of the party. The black man was used as a political tool in the south during the 'carpetbag' regime and temporarily sacrificed his social safety. For thirty-three years he has delivered his vote to the republican party like a poor man gives his pound of flesh to the shylock.

Now we have the spectacle of tin soldier, a flashlight hero [Theodore Roosevelt], whose pen is mightier than his sword, who 'conceived' the idea of rough rider regiment because he had seen Buffalo Bill's Wild West circus. He is saved from death in Cuba by the colored soldiers who rush to the rescue of his "three-sheet" troopers. He returns to the states and poses for emoluments and the camera and writes for the magazines of how he forced the black soldiers to keep to the front at the point of his pistol.[4]

Roosevelt's Insults.

Black men on the battlefield have always been brave. In every war our nation has waged the colored man has shed his blood willingly.

In the war of the revolution, Crispus Attucks, a colored man, was the first to die on Boston common. During the war of 1812 General Andrew Jackson praised the valor of the "men of color" at the battle of New Orleans. Fifty thousand colored men made way for liberty and died in the civil war. The gallant Ninth cavalry rode 100 miles through the blinding snow, Christmas eve, 1891, and rescued the beleaguered Seventh from an Indian massacre. They fought and died in Cuba, and nursed the fever-stricken soldiers at the risk of their lives. And they are now forced to fight their own colored people in the Philippines. All this they have done for their country's sake, and it is left for this vitascope character, this modern Don Quixote, Roosevelt, to accuse my people of being cowards.

---

4. Roosevelt initially gave credit to the African American "Buffalo soldiers" for winning the battle atop Kettle Hill. When he returned home, however, Roosevelt changed his story, claiming that the victory resulted not from the Black soldiers' heroism but from of the leadership of their white officers. See Le'Trice Donaldson, *Duty beyond the Battlefield: African American Soldiers Fight for Racial Uplift, Citizenship, and Manhood, 1870–1920* (Carbondale: Southern Illinois University Press, 2020).

Cannot Force Their Votes.

If Governor Roosevelt "forced" the colored soldier at the point of his pistol to save his life at San Juan hill, he cannot force the colored voter to save his political life on election day. The colored man will then have chance to say, Vengeance is mine; I will repay."[5]

---

5. Deuteronomy 32:5; Romans 12:19.

Is the Pulpit Equal to the Times?

Delivered at the People's Tabernacle, Atlanta, September 27, 1903

SOURCE: Henry McNeal Turner, "Races Must Separate," in *The Possibilities of the Negro in Symposium*, edited by W. B. Parks (Atlanta: Franklin, 1904), 90–98

In this address, Turner took issue with Rev. H. S. Bradley, pastor of Atlanta's influential Trinity Methodist Church, and his assertion that African Americans enjoyed the same rights and privileges as other US citizens. Turner not only countered Bradley's argument but reiterated that emigration was the solution to the "negro question."

Mr. Chairman—Among the remarks that I shall make on this occasion will be a few in reply to Rev. Dr. H. S. Bradley, who fills one of the first pulpits of Atlanta, and is the pastor of a congregation cultured and refined.

I venerate the distinguished divine, Rev. Dr. H. S. Bradley, scholarly, eloquent, humane, as he is, and I believe he is a Christian gem of the first water. Indeed, I have received a personal recognition from him that I have been accorded by no other white minister in the city of Atlanta, while all have treated me with respect. But it so happens that God made me out of that kind of material which enables me to rise above personal considerations sufficiently to agree with my enemies and differ with my friends when the question at issue requires it. Personal likes and dislikes have nothing to do with my honest opinions.

The learned doctor last Monday night, the 21st instant, delivered an elegant and rhetorical speech before a mass meeting of my race (and I was present) against the separation of the races—I mean the white and black races, or, as the Africans say, the Buckra man and the Otutu man. He hurled his florid remarks against negro emigration, segregation, any form of separation or any movement that would contemplate negro concretion, civilly or politically, and as I saw it presented one of the most eloquent and illogical addresses I have heard for a great while—not because he is wanting in logical ability and attainments, for I have heard him both in the pulpit, on the platform, and have read after him, but because he was handling a subject which he had never studied with a view of its practical results, as the early history of Rome, of North America, of South America and of Australia, and indeed the history of all peoples and nations would have shown the folly of his position. For emigration is the philosophy of ancient and modern history.

The bulk of white men know but little about the inner feelings and idio-syncrasies of the negro, and when they speak about black men emigrating to better their conditions they signally fail by reason of the fact that it is not a question that concerns them enough to give it deep and protracted thought. I know there are many white men who ride into popularity by pretending to know all about the negro, but they only know the ignorant and scullion side of him.

In this country, where white represents God, and black the devil, little thought is given to the black man's future. Everything that concerns the negro is whittled down to the present contingencies, and the eternal future which involves and comprehends change, revolution, mutation and the mighty destiny of races, is but little thought of, and if the negro does not think about it himself, it will receive but little attention and our status as a race, to use the language of the elder Judge Lumpkin,[1] is so ignoble, and the foolish scarecrow of social equality has become such a hobgoblin with the ignorant masses, that we are further apart in spirit and sympathy than heaven and hell. We are as ignorant of each other as races as if we did not live in the same world. The very conditions that surround and confront us forbid a white man from

---

1. Joseph Henry Lumpkin (1799–1867) served as the first chief justice of the Georgia Supreme Court (1846–67).

having any real knowledge of the negro, and I could bring a hundred illustrations to establish this fact. It was verified the other night in Dr. Bradley's address when he said the negroes were American citizens, and do not wish to be segregated. I grant that the doctor represented a large portion, for as the Savannah News says, "The negro is not yet a nation building race," but if he will put a steamer between here and Africa and make the rates of travel as cheap as white emigrants get from Europe to America 4,000,000 will leave as soon as they can adjust their little affairs. While I am not burdened to death with intelligence, I have too much sense to say that all would go. I do not know as half would go. Jahn in his Biblical archaeology[2] says that not half of the children of Israel ever left Egypt for the promised land, but the vast multitude which remained has never been heard of from that day till this. No people in the world's history, who were not self-reliant and who are not prompted by their inner nature to sue for better conditions, have ever reached the plane of respectability. Indeed, they are invariably crushed out of existence and exterminated. I have been reading history for over fifty years and if there is any exception to this rule, outside possibly of the Saxons who were absorbed, and also did much of the absorbing by virtue of being of the same color and having the most beautiful women on earth at that time, I would be pleased to have them pointed out.

The doctor says the negro is an American citizen. I wish he was correct. Twelve millions of colored people of the United States would throw their hats, parasols and umbrellas heaven high, if possible, if his declaration about the citizenship of the negro was a reality, or could be established. Surely the doctor has not been apprised of the fact that the conclave in Washington, D. C., called the United States Supreme Court, has issued a legislative decision taking away every vestige of his civil rights,[3] and in the recent Alabama case has declared his political rights a nullity,[4] and outside of the right to pay taxes and work on the roads he has not a single right that would prompt him to be a man. I would mention the degradation this decision, or these decisions (for there are three of them), have inflicted upon the negro, in detail, but it

---

2. Johann Jahn, *Jahn's Biblical Archaeology*, trans. Thomas C. Upham (Andover, MA: Flagg and Gould, 1823).

3. *Plessy v. Ferguson* (1896), in which the US Supreme Court decision upheld the legality of "separate but equal" facilities for white and Black Americans.

4. *Giles v. Harris* (1903), in which the US Supreme Court upheld an Alabama law providing that anyone registered to vote before January 1, 1903, was registered for life, while others would have to pass tests given by local election officials.

would be too voluminous and do no good; but I will give $500 if any man will show me such a decision from any court of last resort in the history of the world. Its uniqueness stands in the fact that they legislated and decided at the same time. No instance of the kind is found in the chronicles of the nation.

But just at this point I beg to ask the doctor if he could have any respect for a man, or any set of men, who would sit quietly under the condition of things that confront the negro in this country? If he wants to know what I mean, just let him color his face (for white is not a color) and attempt to be a man and a gentleman for one day, and he will understand the meaning thoroughly. We are daily the subjects of comment and misrepresentation. God is charged with folly for attempting to make a man and failing to complete His job, and he is assigned to the realm of inferiority, and yet more laws have been enacted by the different legislatures of the country, and more judicial decisions have been delivered and proclaimed against this piece of inferiority called the negro than have been issued against any people since time began. It would appear that the negro is the greatest man on earth if we are to judge from the judicial decisions in the code books of the country to keep him down.

The Pilgrim fathers did not have to contend with one-half of the legal fetters, but they left the old country and sought a land where they could develop the mighty forces that heaven had implanted in their natures, and the result is a great and powerful people have been developed. Which does the doctor have the highest respect for—the early settlers of Plymouth in Massachusetts and Jamestown, Va., or the docile negro who will not try to help himself?

I have been singled out in this country as the chief factor in the African emigration movement, and as such I believe that I have received all of a hundred thousand letters, some of them containing dozens and dozens of names, who are clamoring for transportation conveniences and cheap rates from this to the land of our ancestors, so they can return to Africa without having to pay their way to New York City, then to Liverpool, England, and then to Africa, which they have to do at present, costing them more on the cars to New York than white people have to pay from Queenstown, Liverpool, Hamburg and other points to come to New York, Philadelphia, Boston, New Orleans and Savannah.

Think of it, 557 steamers, besides sailing ships, are hugging the shores of Africa the year round from Europe, and not one from the United States. These European steamers, carrying to her ports hundreds of millions, if not a billion dollars of commerce annually, and not the worth of a nickel of commerce from the United States. Some of us have been trying for years to get this government to subsidize a ship for mail purposes, and let it serve as a transport for emigration and commerce, as a start to the movement, but up to the present our efforts have been fruitless. President Harrison[5] would have done something, but he was afraid of public sentiment. President Cleveland[6] saw the philosophy of it, but was contending with the Hawaiian question and disposed of it by saying time would make it all right; and time will do it. This nation, or its aggregated people, will either have to open up a highway to Africa for the discontented black man or the negro question will hinder this government.

There will be no peace to the United States as long as the negro question is an issue. Might may hold the scepter and sway legislative and judicial power for a time, and even suppress free speech and tyrannize over the dissatisfaction of a people for a while, but right will step to the front in its own good time and twist the scepter from the hands of might, for the reason that God is right. A United States Senator from a Southern State said to me some time ago: "I am opposed to your emigration agitation, especially about returning to Africa in any numbers. You are keeping up an unnecessary excitement," but finally said: "Remember, Turner, that I am opposed to it as a white man, as your race furnishes us with a cheap and obedient labor; but if I was a negro, I will be d——d if I would not leave this country before the sun goes down."

I do not regard Hon. John Temple Graves[7] as the quintessence of infallibility, especially when he is discussing and commenting upon the intellectual and moral status of my race, as he represented them in some respects, in Chautauqua and Chicago, while he only expressed the current opinion of the white people generally; but the remedy that he pointed out to the American people, in regard to the existing condition of things, in my opinion, and in the opinion of sober thinking people generally, raises him to a national majesty, and makes him the greatest statesman and philosopher in the land. Among the notable and illustrious men of the country Mr. Graves towers above them all. Bismarck[8] never offered to Germany, nor Gladstone[9] to England, a

---

5. William Henry Harrison (1773–1841) served as US president (March–April 1841).

6. Grover Cleveland (1837–1908) served as US president (1885–89 and 1893–97).

7. John Temple Graves (1856–1925), editor of the *Atlanta Georgian*, advocated the removal of African Americans from the United States.

8. Otto von Bismarck (1815–98) is credited with unifying Germany in 1871.

9. Willian Ewart Gladstone (1809–98) served as prime minister of the United Kingdom (1868–94).

wiser measure and a more philosophical proposition, than Mr. Graves has offered to the American people. He is evidently a widely read scholar, a master logician, and has the courage of his convictions, and defies public criticism, when he tells the white and black man in this country they must separate, for separation is the ultimatum, and that alone will bring peace to this nation.

I will tell the black man what Mr. Graves thought, but was reluctant to express. Your very existence depends upon separation. At present there is no Christian unity, much less civil and political unity. A shameful division prevails.

When I speak of separation I do not say that everybody will go or must go. I am only contending that there should be a highway made across the Atlantic (only 3,350 miles from the city hall of New York) for such black men and women as are self-reliant and have those manhood aspirations that God planted in them, and degrading laws will intensify. We are not clamoring for rich men, or men of respectable means. We want smart, energetic and self-reliant men. If Australia could be made one of the greatest countries on earth by penal convicts, who would dare say that respectable colored men could not also build up a nation?

Speech at the Institutional AME Church

Delivered at the Institutional African Methodist Episcopal Church,
Chicago, October 13, 1913

Source: *Chicago Daily Tribune*, October 14, 1913

According to the Chicago Daily Tribune, *when Turner was introduced to the audience of "hundreds of negroes who packed the Institutional church" to hear him speak on October 13, 1913, the "white haired old negro walked slowly forward and bowed in acknowledgment. His gigantic frame is still straight. He treads with the step of a powerful horse, his hands are never still, his voice reaches the most distant corner of the church." Addressing Archibald J. Carey Sr. (1868–1931), an AME minister, political activist, and orator, Turner said, "I'm no good tonight. Dr. Carey, what shall I speak about?" Carey replied, "Speak about the moon, bishop."*[1]

The moon—the moon is a globe that has no light of its own. . . . Some people say there is a man in the moon. There is not. There never has been. If there is, it's a different man from those who inhabit the earth. There is no rain on the moon; there are no bays, no lakes, no crowds.

---

1. For more on Carey, see Dennis C. Dickerson, *African American Preachers and Politics: The Careys of Chicago* (Jackson: University Press of Mississippi, 2010).

There are great and mighty cliffs that rise thousands of feet high and cast shadows on the moon's surface. This is what the people think is the man in the moon—the shadows.

The moon is made of sand and slag and stone. It was thrown out of the earth like the earth was thrown off the sun. The world grows larger every day. Once it was only as big as your finger tip. It was all composed of asteroids at one time. It exploded, and the asteroids went up in space and found orbits of their own.

Mercury has no moon. The earth has only one, Jupiter four; I know, because I've looked at them a thousand times through my telescope before my wife's mother broke it. Saturn has eight moons, shining even in the daytime. Neptune has thirty moons.

Mars is inhabited. I have seen great creatures on Mars that looked like wolves. I have seen great lakes and cañons and chasms. But what I think the greatest wonder of all is the "milky way." I intend to visit the "milky way" when I die.

The white race, . . . is the most wonderful race. It is the meanest race, and the best; the narrowest and stingiest, the most liberal. The white people are the biggest fools and the greatest philosophers. The white race is a race of giants.

Help the white man up, but help yourselves while you are doing it. Let your sons and your daughters go to colleges and schools. Give them opportunities, for the black race needs them.

Slavery was a providential institution, but it was not a divine institution. If it were not for slavery, most of us would not now be here. We'd still be in Africa.

The "Jim Crow" car is coming all over the country. We'll have it in Chicago soon, in New York, in Philadelphia, in every big city in the United States.

There are going to be a lot of hard times coming, mark my words—times that we have not passed through yet. Most of us will be going south again. It will come before you have gone from the earth, but while I am sleeping in my grave my words will still be ringing in your ears.

Index

About the Editor

Credit: University of Memphis

Andre E. Johnson is associate professor of rhetoric and media studies at the University of Memphis. He is director of the Henry McNeal Turner Project, a digital humanities project curating the writings of Bishop Henry McNeal Turner. He was named 2020 Scholar of the Year by the Religious Communication Association.

Also by Andre E. Johnson
No Future in This Country: The Prophetic Pessimism of Bishop Henry McNeal Turner

Made in the USA
Middletown, DE
05 September 2024

60379182R00128